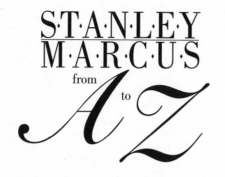

S·T·A·N·L·E·Y
M·A·R·C·U·S
from *A* to *Z*

Viewpoints Volume II

S·T·A·N·L·E·Y M·A·R·C·U·S
from A to Z

Viewpoints Volume II

edited by Michael V. Hazel

University of North Texas Press
Denton, Texas

Printed in the United States of America.

First edition 2000

10   9   8   7   6   5   4   3   2   1

Permissions:

University of North Texas Press

PO Box 311336

Denton TX 76203-1336

The paper used in this book meets the minimum requirements of the American National Standard for Permanence of Paper for Printed Library Materials, z39.48.1984. Binding materials have been chosen for durability.

Library of Congress

Cataloging-in-Publication Data

Marcus, Stanley, 1905–

Stanley Marcus from A-Z : viewpoints volume II / by Stanley Marcus ; edited by Michael Hazel.—1st ed.

p.   cm.

Additional newspaper articles to those published in author's The viewpoints of Stanley Marcus in 1995.

Includes index.

ISBN 1-57441-073-3 (alk. paper)

1. Marcus, Stanley, 1905– Viewpoints of Stanley Marcus. II. Hazel, Michael V., 1948– III. Title.

AC8.M354 2000

070.4'4—dc21   99—53441

Contents

Yesterday

Introduction

In 1984, Burl Osborne, then editor (and now publisher) of *The Dallas Morning News*, asked Stanley Marcus if he would like to write an opinion column for the paper. Once he was assured that he could write on any subject he chose, Mr. Marcus happily agreed, although he declined Osborne's initial proposal of three columns each week, on the grounds, as he explained, "that three a week would be work, whereas one a week could be fun."

Stanley Marcus, of course, is a living legend in Dallas, the arbiter of taste during his tenure at Neiman Marcus, a book man extraordinaire, and the conscience of the community in the opinion of many. Being the shrewd newspaperman that he is, Burl Osborne knew that there was a ready-made audience for anything Mr. Marcus chose to say or write.

And he was proved right. Mr. Marcus's column became an eagerly awaited feature of the Tuesday paper. People stopped him on the street or button-holed him at parties to offer him their reaction to one of his commentaries. This was what Mr. Marcus was after. "If my columns activate readers to read critically," he observed in 1995, "I have accomplished my objective. I don't seek agreement when I write, for my objective is to inform, clarify, expose fresh ideas and stimulate."

After ten years, and some 500 columns, it was apparent that Mr. Marcus had created a substantial body of work. The editors of the University of North Texas Press therefore collected 116 of the columns into a book entitled *The Viewpoints of Stanley Marcus*, which was published in 1995. The book was well received both by critics and book buyers.

But Mr. Marcus didn't see the publication of *Viewpoints* as an excuse to cease his weekly output. He kept writing, and within a few years he had produced a couple hundred more columns. And there were all those earlier ones that hadn't made it into *Viewpoints*.

So another volume seemed called for. But this time, instead of letting the editors of UNT Press make the selections, Mr. Marcus asked me to do so, and I was delighted to accept the invitation. What a treat to sit down and read through sixteen years of columns, one after the other. I rediscovered old favorites, but I also found many more that I had missed on their initial newspaper publication. And reading them as a group made me appreciate more than ever the keenness of Mr. Marcus's insight and the effectiveness of his literary style, to say nothing of the breadth of his interests.

One of Mr. Marcus's strengths is that he can take a subject, and in only 500 to 600 words he can analyze it, provide some anecdotal detail, and round the column off with a punchline that drives his message home. In other words, he knows the value of being concise. He learned the art of brevity, he explains, while delivering a regular 120-second commentary on a local radio station. That lesson he carried over to his newspaper column, to the great benefit of readers and editors alike.

Selecting the columns for inclusion in this book was difficult. Nearly every one held up remarkably well, even those written more than a decade ago. The topics were always interesting, and even when I didn't agree with Mr. Marcus's opinion, I was intrigued by his arguments. My final criteria were few: I eliminated those that had appeared in *Viewpoints*, preferring to devote limited space to columns not previously published in book form; and I eliminated any that might seem "dated" in a few years because they dealt too closely with topical events. Among the remainder, I selected those that seemed to me to display best Mr. Marcus's remarkable wit and wisdom.

Organizing the columns presented an interesting challenge. Arranging them chronologically, in order of publication, as had been done in *Viewpoints*, didn't seem appropriate. Since I had deliberately selected each column because it seemed timeless, *when* it was published was irrelevant (although the original publication date has been listed after each article as a point of reference).

Some sort of topical arrangement seemed better, and at first I thought I might be able to group the hundred-plus articles into ten or twelve general categories. But on closer inspection, I realized that what makes Stanley Marcus's columns appealing to so many people is that he addresses so many different subjects, from body language and book borrowing to marriage and music, and from phobias and printing to weather and writing. Taken together, the columns I selected form a small encyclopedia, into which a reader can dip for insight into a wide range of topics.

So they are arranged alphabetically in no fewer than sixty-two categories.

Now ninety-four years old, as of this writing, Stanley Marcus possibly has shown a sign of slowing down. On second thought, knowing Mr. Marcus it's more likely he's simply changing direction. For in his column of November 2, 1999, he announced he was retiring "from . . . weekly columnist to . . . occasional contributor. . . ." We can only hope he keeps writing occasionally for some time so that early into the new millennium yet a third volume of his collected articles will be justified. For now, I hope *Stanley Marcus from A to Z* will take its place alongside his other works in capturing some of the wisdom of a remarkable man.

Michael V. Hazel

A Compendium of Sage Advice

One of the delights of rearranging books is the happenstance rediscovery of a book you always meant to read or had read and intended to reread. Then your wife straightened the library, shoved the book back in the case, and said book became forgotten or unfindable.

This happened to me this past week when I had the good fortune to rediscover a book called *The Official Rules* by Paul Dickson. I have no idea whether it is in print or not, but it should be. If you have an interest in trivia, it's worthwhile getting a copy to be regaled by the collected wisdom of the authors of the various rules on virtually any and every activity in life.

It is a compendium of information on just about everything that matters, like Gen. Creighton W. Abrams' advice, "When eating an elephant, take one bite at a time," to Zymurgy's *First Law of Evolving System Dynamics*, which says, "Once you open a can of worms, the only way to recan them is to use a larger can (old worms never die, they just worm their way into larger cans)."

In a society where laws are constantly being violated by criminals, being evaded by bureaucrats, being appealed by litigants, being flouted by arbitrageurs, it is comforting to find a book containing laws that are immutable and not subject to either divine or human challenges.

Such as *Loevinger's Law*, which postulates, "Bad news drives good news out of the media," or *Kirkland's Law*, which states, "The usefulness of any meeting is in inverse proportion to the attendance," and *Jacquin's Postulate on Democratic Governments*, which says, "No man's life, liberty or property is safe when the legislature is in session."

There is some sage advice in many of these laws, which, if observed, will simplify the process of life. One of them is *Harris' Law*, which states, "Any philosophy that can be put in a nutshell belongs there." Another is *Hackett's Law*, which reads, "The belief that enhanced understanding will necessarily stir a nation or an organization to action is one of mankind's oldest illusions."

Along with those bits of wisdom you will discover some very simple principles relating to human behavior, like *Dibble's First Law of Sociology*, "Some do, some don't," and the *Dieters' Law*, "Food that tastes the best has the highest number of calories," and *Diogenes's Second Dictum*, "If a taxpayer thinks he can cheat safely, he probably will."

Contributions to a better understanding of our fellow men and women range from *The Law of Characters and Appearance*, which postulates, "People don't change; they only become more so," to *Clopton's Law*, "For every credibility gap there's a gullibility fill," and to the *Farmers' Almanac Computer Maxim*, which says, "To err is human, but to really foul things up requires a computer."

There's *Concoroni's Law of Bus Transportation*, which will interest DART officials as well as bus riders in the Metroplex. It states:

• The bus that left the stop just before you got there is your bus.

• The amount of time you have to wait for a bus is directly proportional to the inclemency of the weather.

• All buses heading in the opposite direction drive off the face of the earth and never return.

• If you anticipate bus delay by leaving the house thirty minutes early, your bus will arrive as you reach the bus stop or when you light up a cigarette, whichever comes first.

• The last rush hour express bus to your neighborhood leaves five minutes before you get off work.

• Bus schedules are arranged so your bus will arrive at the transfer point precisely one minute after the connecting bus has left.

• Any bus that can be the wrong bus will be the wrong bus. All others are out of service or full.

2

Finally, immodestly, I must quote *Marcus Law* from my book *Quest for the Best*, in which I lay down a rule for business success by stating, "Never divorce the boss's daughter (or son)."
September 8, 1987

ટ્ર

Advice to the Third Generation

Dear Pamela:

When you came to my office seeking some career counsel, I couldn't help but recall that a scant thirty years ago your mother had visited me seeking similar advice. It reminded me of that choice Yogi Berra comment, "This is deja vu all over again."

And so it is. You don't look like your mother, but you have some of the same facial and vocal mannerisms. You weren't consciously aping her, but her influence has been absorbed into your lifestyle, as it well should be, for you have been her genetic inheritor.

I have a pretty fair sense of recall, so I do remember a few of the things I told your mother in the early '60s, some of which she accepted immediately, others on which she postponed action until a later day, and many which she rejected for a variety of good reasons.

All in all, my box score proved to be pretty good with her, although she did decide to marry before she was really ready for the experience. But as Yogi Berra might also have declared, "You can't win them all, because it's tough to think and hit at the same time."

Before I proceed any further, I want to explain why I am writing this letter. Since you are twenty-three, it is not only improbable but impossible that I will be around to counsel with a third generation in your family. Thus this letter, which I hope will find its way to your daughter's or son's hands at the proper time.

Advice is perishable, I know, so what I may suggest to you today may have no relevance to your offspring, but please put up with my vanity as I try to establish myself as a three-generation family adviser.

I recommended to your mother that she seek a career in business, for in the early '60s, business was just becoming aware of the potential contribution to the top levels of management that women might make. I also told her that her success would not depend so much on her physical attractiveness, but rather upon the coincidence of her intellectual acuity. I urged her to go to a graduate business school, which she eventually did.

When you came to see me, inspired perhaps by nice things your mother had to say about me, you posed a very direct question on how best to maintain your language skills while working in this country. I replied very flatly that there was little likelihood that you would find a position here that could benefit from your language accomplishments unless you chose a teaching or translating job.

"If that doesn't appeal to you, then go back to Italy, and I'll send introductions to people in the fashion industry who should be interested in a bright, fashionable, young American woman who speaks Italian in the vernacular." Evidently that was the advice you wanted, for you had departed before the signatures on my letters were fully dried.

I repeat, "If you follow my counsel to learn as much about the companies to which you are going to apply, and if you remember to carry a shopping bag bearing the imprint of your prospective employer, I rate your job chances as excellent. Above all, overwhelm them with your knowledge and enthusiasm, and don't forget what I imparted to you about Italian men."

Now, as to the third generation, I feel some security in projecting a forecast, for human nature isn't going to change one iota between now and 2014. However, there will be some new ways of doing old things that may or may not be better, but they will be new and will deserve a trial.

In the 21st century, intellectual integrity will be a prime requisite, and simply stated, that means not being a phony. Learn your school and college subjects well enough to know them thoroughly and exhaustively. I foresee that in the 21st century there will be less tolerance for second-raters, simply because there's going to be increased competition from people from all parts of the world. What you are will be more important than who you are, or from where you came, or your color.

By that time, I hope there will have been a revival of parental authority, and that the education system of the '90s will have been so repudiated and so renovated that your generation will be better prepared to accept your role in adulthood than existed at a similar time in your parents' lives.

And as for who is this Yogi Berra I've quoted, we'll just leave it at this: He was a 20th-century philosopher who also happened to play baseball.

April 2, 1991

GING

How to Tell You're Aging

Recently, a friend sent me a single-spaced, typed sheet titled "Aging Is When . . ." Unfortunately, the author was unidentified. His understanding of geriatric problems and attitudes was acute, and he deserves recognition. The piece started off by saying, "Aging is when everything hurts, and what doesn't hurt, doesn't work."

The piece went on, "Aging is when the gleam in your eyes is from the sun hitting your bifocals; aging is when you feel like the night after, and you haven't been anywhere; aging is when your little black book contains only names ending in M. D."

It continued, "Aging is when you get winded playing chess, when your children begin to look middle-aged, when you finally reach the top of the ladder and find it leaning against the wrong wall, when you decide to procrastinate but never get around to it, when your mind makes contracts your body can't meet, when you know all the answers but nobody asks you the questions, when you look forward to a dull evening, when you walk with your head high trying to get used to those bifocals, when your favorite part of the newspaper is '25 Years Ago Today.'

"It's when your knee buckles and your belt won't, when you regret all those mistakes resisting temptation, when you're 17 around the neck, 44 around the waist and 96 around the golf course, when you stop looking forward to your next birthday, when dialing long distance wears you out, when you're startled the first time you are addressed as an 'old-timer,' when you just can't stand people who are intolerant, when you burn the midnight oil until 9 p.m., when your pacemaker makes the garage door go up when you watch a pretty girl go by, and when you get your exercise acting as a pallbearer for your friends who exercise."

This opus ends with, "Aging is when you have too much room in the house and not enough room in the medicine cabinet," to which observations I would add from my own experience, "It's when the antics of a two-year-old child or a puppy cease to be as amusing as they were twenty years ago. It's when people you haven't seen for a few weeks remark on how well you look."

Apparently, the easiest conversation to make with aging friends is to comment on their physical appearance, as if the fact their faces haven't sagged or turned color since the last meeting is newsworthy.

The best antidote to aging for those in good health is to stay active and retain a participating interest in the world. Life is too exciting and interesting to retire from it. Tackling new problems appears to be a good prescription to stimulate the brain cells and maintain good health.

September 22, 1987

ৰ

"Physically Challenged" Tells It Like It Is

Inflation has affected not only prices but also the simplest of titles as well. Inflation has turned the honest "janitor" into a "sanitation engineer" and the "personnel manager" into the "director of human resources." It has also come up with one new term that I approve of for a change.

Lately I've been hearing the word "challenged" to describe the physically handicapped. This seems to me to be a much more accurate term, as any of us who have ever had to cope with a broken bone can attest. Having recently suffered a broken ankle, I'm speaking from personal experience, not theory.

Even such a temporary handicap leaves one astonished at the amount of physical and mental energy it takes to get on with the little chores of living that we normally take for granted. Just getting up, getting dressed and off to work becomes an exercise in logistics that looms on a par with Gen. George Patton's march through France and Germany. We're irritable from the pain and our lack of mobility, so we snap at friends and family just when we need their support most.

Then, there's the feeling of loss of self-esteem, nonetheless real for being irrational, as we lumber along on clumsy crutches, or walkers, helpless to negotiate a door without help. And while well-meaning friends make jokes about our disability as they sign the cast, we feel a flash of anger even as we laugh along with them. Underlying all the pain, the inconvenience and the frustration is the unpleasant reminder of our own mortality. To think that such a tiny twist of a normally reliable limb was enough to break it! Although my major inconveniences lasted only a few months, it has given me a lifetime of respect for the physically challenged.

Walking is serious business, and I, like others, have been guilty of paying too little attention to the mechanics of the activity. My accident occurred at a garden party where I had my foot in my mouth instead of on the ground as I was negotiating a step. My foot became entangled in a camera strap, and I stumbled. Both the owner of the camera case and I were equally culpable.

The "twisted ankle" turned out to be a broken one which required the wearing of a cast for several months. The greatest problem I faced was sleeping with my foot encumbered in a weighty cast, which acted as an anchor, causing me to strain my back as I turned in my sleep.

During this austere ordeal, I was impressed by the helpfulness and courtesy of people I didn't know, who opened doors, assisted me on and off planes, and encouraged me to be of good cheer.

The experience has given me new respect for those with permanent disabilities. That the permanently disabled overcome anger, depression and frustration to lead whole and productive lives is a daily miracle we should all remember not to overlook.
July 3, 1990

Growing Old Can Be Fun

In John le Carre's excellent new book, *The Secret Pilgrim*, I came across a phrase, "you only grow old once," which reminded me of the experience I am currently enjoying.

My mother, who lived to be 97, told me in response to my inquiry as to how she maintained such a vigorous attitude toward life, "I try to tackle new subjects that I have to study to be able to deal with them; I try to avoid the repetition of activities with which I am familiar, for they don't expose me to fresh and new ideas."

When I asked whether she had many aches and pains at her age, she confessed, "Of course I do, but you can't get to my age without them; I have learned not to talk about them; nobody is interested."

I have observed and practiced those two pieces of advice. Learning something new every day is an objective I set for myself, and it has worked well for me just as it did for my mother. Fresh problems create fresh challenges; the acquisition of new ideas seems to have a therapeutic effect not only on the mind but on the body as well.

That may be the reason why retirees who play golf every day find that life gets duller and duller for them. True, each stroke may be a fresh experience, but it is unlikely to stretch the mind as much as a new piece of learning. Tackling a fresh, physical activity may be more stimulative than the repetition of a series of body actions that have been done a thousand times before.

When I started my consulting business, I sought clients who were not retailers in order to learn about new fields of endeavor. I've done work for shopping center developers, national advertising agencies, and the transportation and communication industries.

I must admit, though, that my retail schooling has proved to be an ideal educational background, for it has provided me with a wide range of experiences in everything from psychology to marketing, strategic planning to personal leadership. Retailing is an industry with possibly the broadest perspective of the world in general and people in specific. It is a business that requires quick decision making, and an optimistic appraisal of fellow men. When practiced properly, it is loaded down with common sense, which I suspect may be the scarcest of the senses.

Getting back to Mr. le Carre's phrase, I am making the most of it. I live a very active, busy life. I enjoy my family and friends, I explore new ideas daily, and through this column, I am able to express myself by the written word. As an octogenarian, I can admit that I'm having a ball; my second career provides almost as much satisfaction as the first one. I was reminded of what Noel Coward once said, "Sometimes work is more fun than fun."

April 23, 1991

ॐ

Age Is Not Important

When I was visiting in Switzerland this past spring, I selected a luncheon spot at the lake's edge in Lucerne. It was not an elegant restaurant, but a simple, slightly touristic spot, serving typical Swiss dishes, such as a cheese fondue and those delicious "Appenzellers," veal bratwursts, named for the town of Appenzell, famous for its superb hand embroidery.

I ordered the bratwurst with rosti, and while I was waiting to be served, I glanced at my paper place mat, which was imprinted with a bold sentence in German. My German is fairly elemental, but I succeeded in translating it into English. It reads: "AGE IS NOT IMPORTANT UNLESS YOU ARE A CHEESE."

It was a relationship I had not considered previously. Only in Switzerland would cheese be considered the discriminating word. In France, "wine" would have been chosen, and in Britain, the

10

word "scotch" would have been substituted. In the United States, in all probability, it would have been "under age."

There are a lot of people who will disagree with the major proposition. The young, for example, aren't a bit satisfied with being young, as they should be. The middle-aged are not happy, as they begin to gain weight, and their clothes get tight; they want to return to the joys of youth as they remember them. Age and aging are significant problems to this group.

Senior citizens enjoy discounts on airplanes and streetcars, but that doesn't compensate them for the aches and pains of arthritis, muscular stiffness, and impairment of hearing and sight. Many older people are going to cogitate about the importance of age and will start comparing themselves with a cheese, a bottle of wine or a quart of scotch. They'll probably eliminate the scotch, for that product doesn't get any better or worse with age. Its development ceases the moment it leaves the cask.

In the right temperature, cheese ripens quickly, but out of the fridge, it spoils faster and smells; whereas wine improves with age—even after it's in the bottle—up to a point. Then it becomes vinegar. It gets tired and gives up the battle. On reflection, I guess that's what happens to people as well.

Humans are more like wine than cheese. Many of them also improve with age; some have a relatively short life. Some develop a patina; some, like wines, get a little fruity. Some grow a little and then remain static; others, like the great vintages of Burgundy, have a long life and get better and better and become more enjoyable as they mellow.

I'm having my own set of mats printed with the message: "AGE IS NOT IMPORTANT UNLESS YOU ARE A WINE."
July 30, 1991

Being Liked: The Ultimate Compliment

One cannot arrive at one's 90th birthday without having met and known a lot of people. And when one has been in a public-oriented business, such as retailing, one's acquaintanceship expands even further.

Any old ship attracts barnacles; I have many. One bit of evidence is that my office Rolodex has reached close to the 3,000-name mark in the twenty years I have been out of active retailing.

It is a nice experience to run into someone whose grandmother from Waco used to bring her grandchildren to the store during the Depression for a day's shopping for back-to-school clothes, or a bride whom I counseled on the selection of a wedding veil, or a man who purchased successive mink coats for his three wives during a thirty-year period.

It is warming to share their pleasant shopping recollections, which have remained bright in their minds. On balance, I guess most of them had satisfactory business relations with me, for none recounted anything but incidents that reflected happy memories.

I feel I am the possessor of a large bank of public goodwill, which is one of the nicest things that can happen to anyone. When a stranger, either man or woman, approaches me in a theater lobby and simply says, "I like you," that is an accolade worth its weight in gold.

I may have offended some from time to time, when I have espoused causes or supported political candidates they did not particularly like. On balance, however, I believe I must have earned respect for the integrity of my actions, which were in support of programs in the public interest. That is most gratifying.

The four boys who were tossed out of a Dallas high school in the 1980s because they insisted on wearing shoulder-length hair—and whom I supported in their legal fight—are now engaged in respectable occupations in law enforcement, the clergy and retailing.

My public has forgiven me for supporting John F. Kennedy in his campaign for the presidency, although I suspect some still might vote against him if he were running today. This merely demonstrates that in the heat of controversy, it is easy for any of us to lose perspective with those who disagree with us.

The latest encounter with my distant past came last weekend when an elderly lady and her husband approached me to relate a story that had disappeared from my memory.

On a visit to the home of a cousin, the couple had need for a knife to open a package. The cousin said, "Wait a minute, and I'll get the knife Stanley Marcus gave me when I sat in front of him in . . . the second grade."

"How did he happen to give it to you?" she was asked. "Well, he kind of liked me," she replied. I must have been about eight years old.

Although I have no recollection of the incident, I think it goes to show that I started out liking girls at an early age. As a matter of fact (if the story is true, and I have no reason for doubt), it shows that knives were taken to school even in 1913 and that I might have been charged with sexual harassment—even at that tender age!

April 18, 1995

# ODY LANGUAGE

The Unspoken Language

Experienced salesmen take leads from the body language of prospective customers. Likewise, football and baseball coaches watch for such clues as they study quarterbacks and pitchers in their respective games.

All of us unconsciously drop tips as we go about a host of activities—the way we touch a sweater, examine the dashboard of an automobile in a dealer's showroom, glance at the desserts in a restaurant.

We are constantly giving off signals, but, as with a foreign language, only those who watch can understand what is being suggested by body movements.

A quarterback's foot placement and eye movement can lead to a quick deduction that he is going to pass to the left instead of the right. A prosecuting attorney reads the witness for signs that may reveal whether he is telling the truth.

Many of these signs are involuntary hand or foot motions, eye glances, facial grimaces, or nose twitches. An observer trained in interpreting such actions is able to convert the knowledge to practical purposes. Those who don't understand the language lose a valuable tool in converting a looker into a buyer, or a winning play into a losing one for the opponent.

One of the most commonplace situations in which body language is used is the sign of attraction or rejection given off by lovers. This is fairly obvious, for it is played out both instinctively and accidentally by the participants.

We all have seen looks of lust, demonstrations of affection and simple acts of fondness as people meet on the street or at private parties. In many cases, an astute observer can predict the outcome with a fair degree of accuracy.

One of the nicest of all the body language signs, it seems to me, is that of two people holding hands as they walk down the street. This suggests there is mutual, reciprocated interest, with overtones of human warmth, not necessarily evidences of passion. It says, in effect, "We like each other."

One can see 6-year-olds walking to school together with clasped hands, or young lovers with hands intertwined. What particularly pleases me is when I witness a couple of oldsters, long past active lovemaking, who still have a sufficient residue of fondness for each other to enjoy the simple act of holding hands as they saunter through a mall or sit through a movie.

If you haven't held hands lately, try it; you'll like it!

February 14, 1995

A Book Borrower Is a Pest

Anatole Broyard, a literary critic for *The New York Times*, wrote an interesting article in the *Times* book review section on the subject of lending books. He was concerned by numerous requests from friends to borrow books.

He wrote, "My friends come to me to borrow books because I have more than most people. In their innocence, they have no idea what I go through in lending a book. They don't understand that I think of myself as offering them love, truth, beauty, wisdom and consolation against death. Nor do they suspect that I feel about lending a book the way most fathers feel about their daughters living with a man out of wedlock."

I share Broyard's dilemma, for I, too, am beset by similar requests. If it is for a book that I like, I hate to see it leave my library, for there is rarely a timetable for a lent book's return. Most of the time, the book will be gone two or three months because my friends never consider borrowing with the same degree of importance as I regard book lending. Often I make notations in the margins of books, and I am somewhat reticent to share them with another reader. I take books seriously; many of my would-be borrowers are simply looking for time-killers.

Broyard goes on to say, "Not many of my friends are poor, and thus the questions arise: If you truly wish to read this book, if you are serious, why don't you go out and buy it? Why don't you make the same offering to literature that you make to other good causes?" Frequently, I am asked to recommend a book to others. This is a highly dangerous business; it's somewhat akin to arranging blind dates.

Those who can afford to buy books, but borrow them instead, are depriving themselves of the great joy of visiting the most interesting retail stores of all—the book stores, where they can browse to their heart's content, picking up gratuitous bits of knowledge by the process of sampling a paragraph here and a page there.

Additional compensations in book ownership give the reader the privilege of annotating his volumes, the opportunity of revisiting them years later, and the warmth of recollection of pleasure by seeing the books on the shelf.

Visitors to my library often ask, "How do you keep up with your books?" My reply is, "The study of bookkeeping has taught me an important lesson: Never lend them."

February 25, 1986

Our Brain: the Best Computer

We spend a lot of time these days examining new computers and software packages that come to the market almost daily. They gain paeans of praise from the computer experts, but rarely do we hear a cheer for the human brain, which is the source of all the electronic devices.

The brain is actually a super computer. In addition to exercising its functions that direct most human activities, it serves as a remarkable storehouse and reservoir of human experiences.

It records impressions and experiences we have in our daily lives with other people, institutions such as banks, stores, utilities, restaurants, hotels and even movies. It stores this information, good and bad, for an unlimited duration. Then on command, ten or twenty years later, it issues a memory recall, though not a hard copy, of our reactions to the state of satisfaction a given service gave us, together with a recollection of the quality of service or product, and even through our smelling reactions.

On the basis of these favorable or unpleasant recollections, we are aided in making current decisions, as to whether to return for a repeat visit or purchase. If the past record shows a green light, we return. If it's red, we go elsewhere.

Now, an expert in brain functions may criticize this layman's explanation of one of the remarkable operations of the brain as being trivial and unscientific. Admittedly, it pleads guilty to being non-technical. There is no attempt here to explain how the brain works, but rather to spotlight the remarkable information source we have for helping us make decisions.

Businesses lose potential purchasers because, by acts of

commission or omission, the impressions are registered in the brain's memory bank. This means that anyone who deals with the public must be constantly aware of the importance of every transaction, for they are recorded. There's no margin for error. The human brain will often forgive, but it rarely forgets a good or bad experience.

The best advice to sellers and purveyors of services is to remember that some of your customers may be doing business with you today for the first or last time. If you take good care of your customers' first experiences, they'll give you the opportunity of making the last sale.

Let's hear it for the human brain.

February 16, 1993

ROMIDES

We Take Bromides to Heart

One of the bromidic proverbs we constantly quote to one another is, "You can't get something for nothing." Another is, "There's no such thing as a free lunch." Have you ever stopped to wonder why? Maybe we don't really want to know.

Several years ago, Maryln Schwartz, one of my favorite writers for this newspaper, focused my attention on this fascinating insight into human nature.

She related a story about an auto dealership bordering one of the busiest freeways in Dallas that had a big, computerized sign that flashed messages to passers-by. For years, it communicated the personal philosophy of its owner, Ed Doran. There were noncommercial messages to brighten the motorists' day, such as, "Never trust a skinny cook."

Naturally, since almost 200,000 people passed the sign every day, it had great influence as an advertising medium. Would-be advertisers constantly approached Mr. Doran with lucrative offers to rent space on his flashy billboard. But he refused, pointing out that the space wasn't for sale.

Then one day, Mr. Doran had an idea: Why not give away the space? He bought large ads in the newspaper, inviting anyone to submit a message and promising to run the most clever or most informative ad absolutely free for one day.

He expected a deluge of response. What he got was practically nil. Plenty of people wanted to pay for the sign, but almost nobody wanted it for nothing.

The story brings to mind another of our favorite proverbs: "You get what you pay for." Apparently, we have taken it so much to heart that we extend the meaning to say, "What you don't pay for is worthless."

We all have had some disastrous experiences with so-called bargains. We are skeptical of "free" offers, because, generally speaking, they turn out to be expensive rather than free. That leads us to scrutinize bargain offers to determine if there are any unrevealed conditions to the offers or defects in the products.

While we may not want something for nothing, we still are ready for a genuine bargain. Mr. Doran might have gotten plenty of takers if he had offered his sign for 50 percent off—this week only.

January 17, 1995

CHANGE

Colliding with Change

The current generations have witnessed and participated in more change than any ten previous generations combined. While we enjoy, to greater or lesser degrees, the changes brought by TV, power brakes, new medications, airplanes and telephonic services, the impact of change itself is disturbing to many.

The way we bank, entertain, travel and conduct our daily lives has changed as new methodologies for all of those activities evolve and become standardized procedures. And what's more, they are going to continue to change well into the next century to even greater degrees than we have experienced so far.

Take retailing, for example, since that is a subject with which I have had direct involvement. We are at the threshold of TV marketing of all types of commodities. By 2000, there will be scores of TV shopping programs, most of which will bear little resemblance to the crude sales pitches that are currently on the air.

Some will be successful, but the majority will fall by the wayside. Those that survive the competitive war will bring new shopping conveniences to their customers. Will they affect catalogs? Yes, for they will provide many of the conveniences of catalog shopping but with greater immediacy of service.

Will the TV shopping programs replace stores and shops? That isn't likely, although they may transfer 10 percent to 15 percent of the total retail business. They won't take away enough volume to replace stores, but enough to force stores to adopt new techniques to survive the increased competition.

Customers find the present state of retailing puzzling. Some retailers are equally puzzled. What we are seeing is a vast expansion of the production of consumer goods. The world is making more goods than buyers can consume. That oversupply leads to constant repricing in order to move the merchandise.

We are geared to handle a flood of products at stable pricing only when there is sufficient buying power to absorb it. The minute buying power drops or supply increases, we witness distress selling, such as when department stores try to stimulate purchases through sales, bonuses or other inducements.

Some stores are battling antiquated locations. They find themselves in difficult competitive situations and have to price more aggressively than competitors that are located where the majority of customers want to shop.

The discount stores maintain the pressure with daily lowest prices, while the specialty stores provide the most customer services and conveniences. Meanwhile, the department stores, caught in the middle with large physical capacities, find themselves in a constant state of repricing.

There are some who believe the department stores will have to be renovated to meet the challenges of the next century. If that happens, it won't be the first time an established and respected industry has been forced to meet the realities of change.

March 14, 1995

6 OLLECTING

Grandmother Was Right

Almost every columnist, it appears, feels obligated to do a piece on one or both grandmothers, who usually appear to be the patron saints of grandchildren. They are universally identified as having infinite wisdom and an ability to understand children far surpassing that possessed by parents.

My maternal grandmother filled to perfection the role that I have just described. It was she whom I went to for advice when I was in conflict with my parents. It was she who impressed upon me the importance of a good conscience, without which, "one could not sleep peacefully." It was she who preached the value of frugality and all the commonplace virtues.

I think of her often, but recently her memory was vividly recalled when my wife purchased several magazines listing antiquities and miscellaneous collectibles for sale. I had been aware that such publications existed, but I never had occasion to examine them carefully.

A review of them convinced me that eighty years ago my grandmother had foreseen that, eventually, there would be a market for anything. She was so economical that she never threw anything away, including string, which she rolled up into balls, as well as bottles of all varieties, and numerous other items that most people, even before the age of super abundance, would have tossed away.

She did not envision that there would be national organizations dedicated to the collecting of everything from old watches to comic books, from old telephones to pins, and from buttons to bottle caps.

This fad of collectibles is a vast industry today. Thousands of dealers are concentrating in minute areas of interest, and hundreds of thousands of collectors trade with them and subscribe to the dozens of publications dedicated to specific fields of collecting.

There is a lot of hokum connected with the collectibles industry in which newly made articles are created to fill the national demand for nostalgic objects. But there is also hokum and hyperbole attached to the older and more recognized collecting mania in the fields of paintings and sculpture, furniture, automobiles and books.

Collecting is fun at whatever level a person has an interest and can afford. It is educational and enables lots of nice people to meet others with shared interests. In only rare instances are they as profitable investments as they may be purported to be.

Grandmother was right: Sooner or later, all things will have some use and value, if we just hold them long enough.

October 4, 1994

CRITICS

Criticism of Art Beneficial

Historically, museum directors have lived in glass houses, inviting targets for public scrutiny and criticism. The old cliche, "I don't know anything about art, but I know what I like," is as operative today as it was fifty years ago.

With the increase of public interest in art, museums now find themselves under a spotlight as never before. An exhibition of paintings can be panned as vigorously as a new novel or movie. Both content and presentation are fair prey for the critics.

The Metropolitan Museum's exhibition of the paintings of Vincent Van Gogh was under severe attack by the art critic of *Newsweek* a few issues back because of the manner in which many of the works were hung. Other shows have been praised or criticized on the basis of the freshness of the material, the lighting and the oral commentary (or lack thereof).

Such criticism is beneficial to the museums and to the art-going public alike. It can succeed only in making museum staffs more alert to their responsibility to produce shows that merit public support and interest and in shaping the viewers' eyes and knowledge.

For the moment at least, we are free of the kind of interference that existed in the 1950s when the content of shows was attacked on the basis of art philosophy—that is traditional paintings vs. avant garde paintings—or the artists' political commitments.

Some will remember those sad days of the McCarthy period when a group of self-appointed censors threatened to ban an exhibition at the Dallas Museum of Fine Arts titled "Sports and Art." This show was sponsored by that radical publication, Henry

Luce's *Sports Illustrated*, to raise money to support the American Olympic team's trip to that year's games in Australia.

The complaint leveled by one of Dallas' leading semi-political figures and head of this group was that the names of some of the artists had appeared on the notorious Dondero list of suspected Communists. The fact the charges were never proved did not prevent many innocent artists from having their careers ruined. When a threat or boycott of this show was brought to the attention of publishers of both *The Dallas Morning News* and *The Dallas Times Herald*, both joined forces in making an investigation of the validity of the charges. They found no substance to them and declared his proposed ban was a threat to freedom of expression and a violation of the Bill of Rights, which guaranteed this protection to both individuals and institutions.

They exposed the threats, the exhibition opened on schedule and the protesters failed to carry forth their attempts at intimidation.

That this incident actually took place in Dallas in the 1950s shocks many who weren't even born at the time, or were not residents of this area. It did happen, and could happen again—whenever our society permits the intimidating tactics of a McCarthy to enjoy public respectability, whenever we allow false charges to go unanswered, whenever the techniques of the inquisition replace the standards of our justice system.

Good art, theater and literary critics serve useful purposes; false critics we don't need.

November 6, 1984

CURRENCY

Passing the Dirty Buck

Money launderers aren't the only ones caught with dirty money these days. The average dollar bill in each of our pockets is more tattered and torn than ever before.

What's happened to the nice, crisp, new dollar bills? It's bad enough that the bills have lost a lot of their buying power, but now they look shabbier too. Today, the average dollar bill has a permanent crease through George's nose. It's bent at the corners, torn at the edges, and it's filthy.

No amount of cajoling or kicking will force a luggage cart dispensing machine at an airport to accept a bill like that. You can barely get rid of them in payment for a purchase. Frequently, you end up with a bill in exchange that's in as bad or worse condition.

The *Wall Street Journal* tried to get to the bottom of the dirty money heap. Its investigation showed that small banks blame big banks for the dirty money. Big banks blame the Federal Reserve Board, saying their new sorting system lets bad bills slip by. The Federal Reserve Board blames the member banks. They say the modern-day teller doesn't take the time to sort out bad bills. Instead, they say, she gives them back to her customers. It sounds like a classic case of passing the buck.

One organization that probably isn't to blame is the Bureau of Printing and Engraving. It says money is made of the same high-quality 75 percent cotton and 25 percent linen as always. Frankly, I think inflation is the culprit. The average bill is on the go more these days. I doubt that there are very many bills stuffed into cookie jars and mattresses. People do less holding onto their bills and more passing them on to other people.

Travelers will testify to the fact that currency in England, France, Germany, and Denmark is usually crisp and clean, whereas paper money in circulation in Italy, Spain, Greece and Mexico runs ours a close race.

When one observes the numerous food handlers who touch the food they serve and then the money that is tendered, it's amazing that currency hasn't been labeled by the surgeon general as injurious to the health of its users. Currency must give children a close race as transmitters of bacteria. Someday, some scientist will invent a way of rendering both less dangerous.

In many public eating places in Europe, they have gotten around this problem by requiring the prospective diner to purchase a ticket from a cashier, covering the cost of the food, to present to the server.

The dollar has been through a lot. Its value goes up and down daily; the newspapers are always speculating about it. No wonder a dollar bill looks down in the mouth, but no matter how tattered and torn it gets, no one ever refuses to accept it.

April 14, 1992

 IETING

The Short and Stout of Dieting

The accumulation of excess poundage has been a problem I've fought off and on for the past sixty years. During this period I have lost 400 pounds, and I have personally experimented with each and all of the diets that have had a popular vogue from about 1935 to the present time.

Consequently, I write about diets with some degree of authority. Almost every year a new diet or a variation of an old one has been welcomed by the overweighters. Magazines, particularly the fashion publications, have recognized the public interest in the subject and have discerned that a new diet will do more for good circulation than a new fashion. Some diets have had medical authority to back them up. Others have been concocted without benefit of scientific research.

Most dieters are tempted by programs that promise fast results with a minimum of sacrifice, but weight reduction can be attained only for a price, and that price is a reduction of food intake. Exercise alone won't do the job without concurrent dietary discipline.

Many of the more popular diets attempt to cajole the dieter into thinking he's eating well while dieting. By a skillful use of substitutes for high-calorie foods, and by the decoration of the plates with plenty of parsley, the dieter is persuaded that he is indulging in a Lucullen feast when he sits down to his 500-calorie evening dinner. "Dieting can be fun," "Lose weight overnight," and "Diet and never be hungry" are some of the deceptive lines used to sell a new diet.

Since I've tried them all, I can deny authoritatively that "dieting can be fun" or that it is possible to "diet and never be hungry." Dieting is a bloody bore; it's not fun, and you do get hungry

31

unless you take appetite depressants, which are health hazards. To that I am strongly opposed, because of the side effects I've experienced whenever I've tried them.

For most normal people, successful dieting begins when they have a motive, and for most of them that motive is supplied when they get the devil scared out of them by a physician who lays down the facts of life, that dieting is necessary for a longer life, and then requires his patient to come back at frequent intervals for a weigh-in.

Regardless of which diet I've used, I have discovered a few basic principles, which are essential for me to follow for the duration if I am to meet with any success:

1) **Eat all meals promptly.** The enforcement of this rule requires the dieter to become anti-social, for it rules out dinner parties that are preceded by alcoholic gluttony, which we refer to as "the cocktail hour."

2) **Reduce or eliminate alcoholic intake**—not for the calories consumed, but because alcohol weakens the willpower and leads to temptations.

3) **Destroy the attraction of food and previous eating habits** by boring yourself with monotonous food. Repetitive dishes, such as cottage cheese or eggs, for each meal for two or three days decrease the appetite, whereas well-prepared, small portions of tasty foods simply stimulate the appetite.

4) **Avoid reading cookbooks or looking at food advertisements** during your dieting period. I've gained two pounds simply by reading an issue of *Gourmet* magazine.

My favorite diet cartoon is one by Stan Hunt that ran in the *New Yorker* magazine in 1965: The cartoon showed a diner in a restaurant ordering luncheon, along with the caption, "A cup of carrot juice, one poached egg, a slice of toasted protein bread with half a pat of butter, tea with lemon, half a cup of Jell-O and a (...) damn vanilla wafer."

September 7, 1993

A Discovery That's Worth Living For

In the back of my mind, I have suspected that on my deathbed I would hear a broadcast announcing either that medical scientists had discovered a new and safe medication for the treatment of obesity or that another group of researchers had come up with evidence proving obesity was good for you.

No one has come close to making the latter forecast, but since a hormone has been found to reduce fat in mice, it is hoped that human beings will respond in like manner.

After having spent 80 of my 90 years being food and weight conscious, this is the best news I could have heard. It certainly will stimulate me to try to live long enough to enjoy the benefits of this discovery.

It seems I have been on a diet of one type of another, with varying degrees of success, for most of my life. Name the dieting program, and I am sure I have tried it.

I was an early convert to the Hayes Diet, recommended to me by Karl Hoblitzelle, who was tall and thin. It worked, but its theory was based on the proposition that excess weight was caused by the improper mixtures of high protein and carbohydrate foods, fruits and fats. It required bookkeeper skills to balance a meal, and I never found a good cook who was equally adept at both food preparation and numbers.

I tried the Scarsdale Diet, the Vogue Diet, the Beefeater's Diet, the Grapefruit Diet, the Banana Diet, the Canadian Air Force Diet, the Think Thin Diet, and twenty-five other diets with varying results. My trouble was my inability not only to find a good diet but also to live with one for any lengthy period. My basic difficulty, I am sure, was that there was very little food with which I didn't make friends. I have an appreciation for well-prepared food and a respect for good ingredients.

Some of my happiest moments have been at dining tables at home and abroad. Unlike some people I know, I never ever have forgotten to eat a meal. I wouldn't describe my appetite as gluttonous; it is just regular and dependable.

The prospect now of being able, a few years hence, to emulate these mice who lost 30 percent of their weight without negative side effects sounds like nirvana to me. The scientists forecast that the medication will be fit for humans in a few years. Thus, my hunch that there would be eventual progress in treating the problems of those who are overweight may prove to be prophetic if humans react the way that mice do.

So I am going to try to live until that happy day, when I can eat freely and still be lean and lithesome!

August 15, 1995

REAMS

Use Dreams to Shape the Future

Sometimes it seems to me that the history of mankind is one long process of sink or swim as events and inventions sweep us along in a flood tide over which we have no control.

A growing number of farsighted people are trying to get a grip on our future. We read of "think tanks" where people with brilliant minds pool their expertise and vision to project the various results of the political, economic and scientific paths we're taking. Fortunetelling is no longer a matter of lines on our palms. Computer programs can spit out probable "scenarios" quicker than you can say, "Madame Zola, Reader and Adviser."

Our future is too important to be left to the statisticians and logicians. They can predict based only on a straight-line continuation of the past and present, a pretty sorry prospect. Valuable as such planning is, we need to stop being so logical. The future should be left to the dreamers.

Let's stop saying, "If we continue to do this, we will wind up with that." Instead, let's allow our imaginations to run wild to visualize the best of all possible worlds, not what we think we can get, given today, but what we really want. We could invent a whole rack of futures and try them on like new clothes, selecting the one that becomes us the most.

Nothing's impossible in an invented future, whether the ideal is three cars in every garage or a return to the horse and buggy. Hopelessly optimistic? Maybe so, but there are a number of people who have accomplished things that appeared impossible. It was simply a matter of clearly visualizing what they wanted and then taking the first step.

Business and government alike need fresh approaches to the solutions of old problems, solutions that are based on imagination, unfettered by too many years of experience. The latter is a great quality but only when it is not permitted to interfere with creative thinking.

In my days as a retailer, I was always fearful of the buyer who had been around so long that she remembered too well. She would pass some of the hottest new merchandise ideas because she recalled when something similar had not sold twenty years ago.

Impractical, you say? Think about the foot-scorching summers you spent as a kid, when you wished you could air-condition the whole town. Then think again—the next time you visit your neighborhood shopping mall.

May 29, 1990

&

Alas, Poor Yorick

Successful retailing and show business have a lot in common, and if I hadn't been a retailer, I might have enjoyed being an actor. My urge to play Hamlet isn't nearly as strong, though, as that of one frustrated thespian I heard about.

Some of the most quoted lines in the English theater are in the graveyard scene in Shakespeare's *Hamlet*. In preparing the grave for sweet, drowned Ophelia, the diggers, following the custom of the time, unearth the previous occupant. Hamlet happens along and learns that it is the old court jester, who entertained him as a child. Hamlet seizes the skull and begins his famous speech, "Alas, poor Yorick, I knew him, Horatio . . ."

The next actor of London's Royal Shakespeare Company who plays the role may speak those lines with greater feeling than ever. The skull he'll be contemplating belonged to a great Shakespearian fan of the company, one Andre Tchaikowsky, a

Polish-born pianist. Andre was an accomplished artist in his own right, having won a prestigious piano competition when he was only 19.

Mr. Tchaikowsky nurtured a secret desire to act, having what his friends described as a passionate love for Shakespeare. After becoming a British citizen, he attended performances of the Royal Shakespeare Company as often as he could. It was well that he indulged his pleasure as frequently as possible, for he was fated to die young—at the age of 46.

That's when his friends at the Royal Shakespeare Company discovered that his acting ambition, frustrated in life, would be fulfilled in death. Like Yorick, Andre must have been "a fellow of most excellent fancy" that he should will his skull to the company. "We are honored by this bequest," said the director, who promised that Andre's skull would play Yorick in subsequent productions of *Hamlet*.

Will this thoughtful piece of philanthropy encourage greater acting achievements? Will the presence of the skull of a person impassioned by Shakespeare's words stimulate more thoughtful, more meaningful enunciations of "Alas, poor Yorick . . . "?

Far too many of us have unfulfilled dreams we will never attempt to realize, excusing ourselves with the notion that we're too far along in life to try something new. I salute Andre Tchaikowsky's courageous reminder that it's never too late. Many people are so talented that they can perform well in different professional sports, in painting, as well as in sculpturing and gardening.
February 1, 1994

❧

The Thrill Is in the Chase

When I finished reading Marcel Proust's *Remembrance of Things Past*, seven volumes and 2,300 pages long, I heaved a sigh of relief. I couldn't help asking myself the question, "Was this accomplishment worth the effort it took?"

All of us set goals, dream dreams and pursue the love of our lives. Sometimes, we fall short and feel depressed and disappointed by our failure. But then on occasion, having achieved a goal, we feel depressed and disappointed by our achievement.

When I started the first volume of Proust, determined to read through to the end of the long and difficult novel, I thought that to complete the work would be a satisfying accomplishment. When I finished, I thought, "Oh, that wasn't such a big deal. Maybe I should have read it in the original French."

Proust's works are about a peculiar dissatisfaction we human beings have with our achievements, once they are ours. A folk-wisdom adage expresses the predicament a lot more succinctly than Proust: "The grass is greener on the other side of the fence."

Or "Familiarity breeds contempt." We worship the girl of our dreams from afar and dream of the happiness we would feel if only she were ours. Then the incredible happens, and she returns our love. That is when the insidious little voice inside us says, "She can't be all that special if she'd fall in love with the likes of me."

This feeling, Proust's complaint, must be universal among mankind, since the great religions of the world tell us not to bother accumulating wealth or worldly honors or coveting our neighbor's wife. Yet we continue to be a species of strivers and achievers and occasional coveters. Perhaps it is because of, or in spite of, our suspicion that getting there is not half the fun. It is all the fun.

Along with our Founding Fathers, Proust knew that it is the pursuit of happiness we crave. Blessed are those who yet have a mountain to climb, a symphony to write or a book to read.
January 3, 1995

"Casual" Shouldn't Be Sloppy

For a nation like ours, which pays less attention to a drop in a hemline than the French and Italians, we have given unusual recognition to the adoption of casual wear by a large segment of the male population.

This trend has been evident to fashion observers for some years, but only since the acceptance of a national movement labeled "casual Fridays" has it become a topic of conversation from the boardroom to the coffee table.

The skeptics among us have learned to suspect behind-the-scenes influences whenever a sudden change in manners or habits is propelled onto the public scene. In this case, we should try to identify what group would benefit by a shift in attire.

The most obvious answer would be the men's sportswear industry, its trade associations, the producers of tennis shoes and large retailers that don't possess important clothing operations. They would be likely to have the most to gain from creating a market for sweaters, jeans and sports shirts by making it professionally and socially acceptable to come to work minus a necktie and traditional business suit.

Institutions across the country, including some of the most staid and conservative supporters of the status quo, have yielded to what has the appearance of a spontaneous mass revolution. The popularity of this one-day-a-week surrender to informality has led supporters to demand that it be extended to the entire workweek. And in many instances, business offices have given in.

The idea of suspending dress codes has been better than the execution, for in a preponderance of cases it has led not to more casual clothing but to a standard of sloppiness in attire and attitude as well.

Throughout history, society has maintained standards of propriety, taste and good manners in both human activities and the clothing its members wear. As examples, members of the British bar were required to wear gray wigs as well as judicial robes in court; diplomats and high government officials had their own uniforms of top hats, striped pants and cutaway coats.

Clothing, particularly men's, was designed to distinguish members of the ruling classes, as businessmen were designated, from tradesmen who worked with their hands.

Twentieth-century society has witnessed the end of colonialism, the establishment of independent nations by the scores and a general breakdown in the rigidity of social codes. As we have democratized governments, so have we democratized social standards and the badges of position that clothes provide.

Not all nations have accepted this process with equal enthusiasm or results, nor has the elimination of social imperatives been universally successful.

Cleanliness shouldn't be a victim of casual attire. It is possible to be clean and casual simultaneously. Casual Friday frequently has resulted in soiled jeans and T-shirts that suggest to customers and clients that "we aren't taking things seriously today."

Business executives need to devote some thought to this byproduct of making Friday a relaxing day. Perhaps it would be better simply to stay closed on Fridays.

Women's Wear Daily recently reported on the early days of Willie Brown's term as San Francisco's mayor: "It was the Brioni-suited Brown who spoke out publicly against casual-dress Fridays when he took office in January, ushering in a new sartorial style to the Bay Area."

A male doesn't have to go that far to express a casual appearance. An open collar, a sweater and a jacket with a pressed pair of pants will enable office occupants to indicate their readiness for a relaxing weekend.

March 19, 1996

ℰATING

Chocolate Still Subject of Debate

Chocolate is one of those edibles which we describe as "naughty but nice." Since it is the weakness of thousands, chocolate in any form is frequently described as "sinful." Waiters offering a trayful of chocolate desserts often prelude their presentation with a wink as they say, "This chocolate mousse is free of calories."

It is not so difficult to analyze why we describe some things as "naughty but nice," but why chocolate? What is so naughty about chocolate? It's called a weakness, a passion, and it is sold to us as a delicious sin. Why must we feel guilty to enjoy it?

First of all, it may not be caloric content but chocolate's association with love that renders it a naughty product. Casanova is reputed to have used chocolate as a stimulant for his more reluctant ladies. This theory is buttressed by an old saying, "Tea inspires sentiment, coffee excites the imagination, but chocolate is an aphrodisiac."

In a delightful book titled *Food for Love*, I discovered information that, in the 15th century, Spanish priests prohibited the consumption of chocolate on the grounds that it contributed to wanton and immoral behavior. Thus, chocolate became an official sin sometime in the 1400s, and we have never gotten over it.

Chocolate is still a debatable subject in the 20th century, as evidenced by the recent publication of a newsletter issued by the Princeton Dental Resource Center that states that the consumption of chocolate might be as beneficial to health as an apple a day. The newsletter goes on to report, "So the next time you snack on your favorite chocolate, remember that if enjoyed in moderation, it can be good-tasting and might even inhibit cavities."

To set the record straight, let it be pointed out that the Princeton Dental Center derives its name from its location in the township of Princeton, N.J., and that it is in no way connected with Princeton University or any of its research subsidiaries. In this era of sophisticated scientific research, it comes as a surprise to learn that this "objective" study of the effects of chocolate on tooth cavities was financed by a candy company, M&M/Mars. The newsletter did not reveal this connection.

This attempt by a manufacturer of a product to influence the marketplace by pseudo-scientific research must take its place in the annals of industrial chutzpah with the recent announcement by French researchers that the consumption of two glasses of red wine a day keep the doctor away! Both of these efforts should remind us that centuries ago our predecessors learned that it was unwise to put the fox in the henhouse to serve as a guard.

September 1, 1992

ॐ

New Styles Never Capture Entire Market

In the past twenty years, restaurant food preparation has experienced several revolutions. The first one was "La Nouvelle Cuisine," with numerous claimants declaring they were first to dare to challenge traditional French cooking.

The evidence with the greatest credibility is that Paul Bocuse, in Lyons, was the leader who succeeded in uniting a whole group of young chefs to join with him in this effort. Unlike other revolutions, this one was bloodless; no heads rolled across the cutting block.

The chefs of the new cuisine recognized there was a diner demand for dishes not overweighted with calories or cholesterol. They wanted to be able to eat well without feeling stuffed. Doctors everywhere approved of the change.

That school of cooking substituted oils for butter, reduced the use of heavy cream in sauces, curtailed frying, and then created a whole new style of food presentation. Sometimes artistic design superseded the chef's culinary skill. It's still around, but not as much in evidence as it was.

The second revolution in restaurant food preparation started here in Dallas, when chef Dean Fearing introduced his Southwestern cuisine at the Mansion Hotel in 1985. He recognized a trend toward spicier foods, so he developed menus that glorified the bell pepper and all of the hot little peppers from Thailand and other ports of call along the Pacific rim.

While many Texans liked it hot, it took a year or two before Dean's preparations were enthusiastically accepted. Of course, a restaurant like the Mansion will always season to order if the diner demands milder fare.

Dean's food did catch on, and now Southwestern style is accepted and emulated from coast to coast. So ubiquitous is the bell pepper at the Mansion that it wouldn't be surprising to find a sorbet or even an ice cream made from a combination of yellow, green, black, red and lime-colored bell peppers.

Furthermore, there are many delicately flavored foods like pompano, Dover sole, crab, endive, baby lamb and quail that become sublimated and destroyed by the overpowering peppers. They are too weak to fight back!

One of the first and most costly lessons I learned as a young merchant was that if a new fashion is truly great it may command no more than 20 percent of the public's buying power. I cannot think of a fashion that would be so domineering that the buyers would go 100 percent first, not even 50 percent at the inception, and 100 percent only after it proved its worth in a year or two. Learning to understand that principle was constantly difficult for young buyers to learn. Restaurateurs can benefit from this experience too.

Getting back to food, no one style of cooking will please all of the diners, so it is wise for a great restaurant to provide choice not only in variety of dishes, but in the manner in which they are prepared.

The Romans gave birth to the phrase *De Gustibus Non Est Disputandum*, or "concerning taste there can be no dispute." I have no desire to dispute the taste of those who appreciate the bell pepper more than I do, or the chefs who have exalted this seasoning vegetable to the pinnacle it now occupies in their cuisine. My contention is that those who do not share equal enthusiasm for the hot stuff be given a satisfactory alternative.

To that extent, I would have to rephrase the Latin to read *De Gustibus Est Disputandum* as far as peppers are concerned.

October 1, 1996

Spendthrift Hollywood

In an era when efficiency is extolled as the ultimate object in each industry, the motion picture business stands out prominently for its consistent refusal to curtail its extravagant production methods.

Recently, the *New York Times* reported that the industry was in trouble, as evidenced by the large number of flops of $40 million to $60 million productions during the past year. The *Times* concluded by stating, "Hollywood's new austerity may be more rhetoric than reality."

The motion picture business has had its share of efficiency experts, tightfisted bankers and realistic business executives, but none left a lasting mark on an industry that is suffering from an acute case of narcissism. It likes its glamour and its profligate sex life. It tolerates its dope-using actors, technicians and studio executives. It is in love with its lifestyle. The *Times* observed, "There are doubts that anything short of a tidal wave of red ink for studios will give them the will or the discipline to rein in costs."

Efficiency, if not practiced with sensitivity and keen under-standing, can be very damaging to creative effort; however, there are examples even within the motion picture industry that creativity does not have to be extravagant and wasteful.

Other cultural endeavors have been through this problem with varying degrees of success. As an example, in the '50s, many symphony orchestras found themselves in a fight for survival. In a city that shall be nameless, a member of the business community suggested that the financial problems of the orchestra should be resolved by proven business techniques. He suggested that an efficiency engineer study the operations to identify areas of wasted manpower and money.

This resulting report is being reprinted here to discourage any similar attempts by a new generation that might be misled into believing that there could be hard-nosed corollary between efficiency and the production of art. The orchestra employed a work-study engineer, a specialist in method engineering, from one of the nation's pre-eminent business consulting firms.

After a visit to a concert, he came up with this report: "For considerable periods, the four oboe players had nothing to do. The number of players should be reduced and the work spread more evenly over the whole of the concert, thus eliminating peaks of activity. All the twelve violins were playing identical notes. This seems to be unnecessary duplication. The staff of this section should be drastically cut. If a larger volume of sound is required, it could be obtained by electronic apparatus.

"Much effort was absorbed in the playing of demi-semi-quavers. This seems to be an unnecessary refinement. It is recommended that all notes should be rounded up to the nearest semi-quaver. If this were done, it would be possible to use trainees and lower-grade operatives more extensively.

"There seems to be too much repetition of some musical passages. Scores should be drastically pruned. No useful purpose is served by repeating on the horns a passage which has already been handled by the strings. It is estimated that if all redundant passages were eliminated, the whole concert time of two hours could be reduced to twenty minutes, and there would be no need for intermission."

The conductor agreed with these comments but expressed the opinion that there might be some falling off in box office receipts. The three Bs might come off sounding more like the three Zs.

Even the Japanese have not adopted such efficiency measures. Efficiency in any operation is a desirable goal, as long as it does not destroy the objective itself. It's obvious that, when carried to the extreme, it becomes ridiculous.

46

If and when producers of motion pictures find that the capital investment markets have frozen up because their extravaganzas don't make profits, they will learn that efficient operation has become a necessity. That process is known as "economic determinism." Until then, the *Times* is correct when it concluded that, "Hollywood's new austerity may be more rhetoric than reality."

June 25, 1991

Exercise for Good Health

My father, who was a very wise man in most matters, viewed physical exercise with apprehension and suspicion. As a result, he raised four sons who grew into manhood with little experience in good exercise habits.

We tried golf; we played a little tennis; we learned how to swim, but there was scant parental encouragement for any of these activities. My father reasoned, I believe, that exercise led to accidents and possible broken bones. Therefore, he evidenced little enthusiasm for organized sports, or even unorganized ones. As a result, none of my brothers nor I ever developed any natural athletic prowess. One brother and I played polo, but we never came close to earning a respectable handicap.

Not until I was well into my 80s did I consider making a commitment to a regular exercise regime. That step was brought about by the suggestion of one of my daughters that I might enjoy having a physical trainer come to my house to put me through an exercise program.

This led me to put a priority on a convenient exercise facility when I was forced to move my offices to a new location; I studied the adjacency of spas to the several buildings that I liked and finally decided on one that had excellent facilities within the proverbial stone's throw. I chose that building with the conviction that such proximity would eliminate my last excuse for not becoming a regular attendant.

I established an exercise schedule, and I have given priority to it over all other business matters or counter-attractions. I am there for an hour's workout, three days a week, rain or shine. I started out hating *every* minute of the bicycle, treadmill, weight machines, etc. Now, I have reached the point of hating only *every other* minute.

The compensation, of course, is the wonderful physical and mental exhilaration from sixty minutes of vigorous exercise. This compensation far outweighs the discomfort of the exertion. Obviously, I have missed that sense of enjoyment most of my life, and I regret only that my father discouraged me from recognizing that proper and regular exercise is an absolute essential for healthful existence.

A gymnasium or spa provides the equipment that is helpful in establishing an exercise routine, but I have learned the lesson that all other exercisers have discovered—that the lack of professional equipment is a feeble excuse for not exercising. A single chair or a pair of dumbbells can prove to be acceptable substitutes for sophisticated chrome-plated weight lifts.

The body-building zealots of the '70s and '80s gave exercise a bad name. Most people are not aspiring to the Arnold Schwarzenegger overdevelopment image. All they want is better health through consistent exercise. It took me a long time to learn, but I am glad I found out about exercise in time to enjoy it.

November 9, 1993

We Are Taking Better Care of Ourselves

One of the least-discussed consumer habits of the last half of this century has been the growth in body care through exercise and diet.

It used to be fashionable for women to go on diets, but few ever reached their goals of a 45-pound weight loss. Exercise was limited to eighteen holes of golf or a walk around the block. Even so, dress sizes shrank from 12s and 14s to 4s and 8s.

There was also a time when a salesman in a men's store would refer to a customer as a "48 regular" or a "46 stout," but the number of men who wear such sizes are watching their figures better and are gradually, but surely, getting into shape. Formerly catalog producers would specify photographic models who were 26, 32 or 38 years old. But today, so many men are taking such good care of themselves that a 46-year-old man can have the figure of his 28-year-old son. Age no longer means a size.

Today, through the influence of family doctors and the barrage of newspaper and fashion magazine reports on new diseases, men and women are maintaining serious commitments to good health. The press is entitled to credit for having emphasized to our society that uncontrolled diets are out of date, out of fashion and out of order. The government occasionally has issued bulletins on average weights for people of various heights. Health news makes the front page.

Free enterprise, not subsidized by any government agency, also has succeeded in creating a health care industry with locations throughout the whole city. Manufacturers who have made money on the exercise machines they have created, and operators who have set up physical fitness centers and provided good jobs to college grads who are physical therapists, have made Americans body conscious, as no other sport or competition has succeeded in doing.

A fitness center is a fascinating place to visit simply for observation purposes and study. There are classes for men and women who do aerobic exercises to the latest tunes of the day; some go through the paces on their own as they climb on their Stairmasters that never reach anywhere.

Government regulations or propaganda couldn't make such accomplishments, but the health spas, with an assist from the press, have helped remake a portion of America that is overweight. This isn't a battle won, for it will be with us until that day when an effective control agent is developed without dangerous side effects.

In the past, exercise was available only at the local YMCA or at the gym where prizefighters worked out. Today, there must be hundreds of fitness centers in the city of Dallas alone. They are an inspiration in the success of integration by bringing people of different interests, colors and languages into one pool and one gym to exercise their bodies.

Even the Romans with their plethora of public baths never reached our stage.

August 11, 1998

Is Birth Order Important?

Are second-born children more creative and first-born smarter? A study a few years ago, published in *Parents Magazine*, said so, but I wonder.

I was the first of four sons. My brother Eddie was four years younger. According to the study by Joan Solomon Weiss, that meant I would be serious, shy, sensitive and conscientious. Eddie's birth-order fate would make him relaxed, cheerful, easygoing and diplomatic.

My father would have flatly rejected the notion. He believed, I think, that since his sons all had his genes, they would all turn out to be equal in all ways. My mother probably knew better, but she was meticulous in showing no favoritism or permitting any other member of the family to do so.

Looking back, I was a serious, studious child. My one attempt at creativity was playing the saxophone in high school. My musical career ended when I needed date money to take a girl to my college junior prom and hocked the instrument, thus ending my aspirations to be a lead saxophonist. Eddie, on the other hand, was a fun-loving charmer who floated effortlessly through the math classes that I passed only by great labor.

After graduating from Forest Avenue High School in Dallas, I decided I wanted to go to Harvard, but I failed the college entrance exams. Basically, I was inadequately educated in proper study habits. I was eventually admitted as a transfer student after making acceptable grades as a freshman at Amherst College. Eddie passed the same entrance exam I failed but was asked to leave Harvard because he preferred playing bridge to attending classes. Eddie became a creative bridge player, and I graduated from Harvard with a C-plus average.

Those college experiences had little effect on our respective abilities as retail merchants. Eddie tended to be a little more theoretical, while I may have been slightly more realistic. Eddie provided a valuable quality of imagination of how things would be; I profited from concentrating on accomplishing the achievable.

Customers and staff adored him, for he always had time to sit and talk; I was less adept in "small talk" and gave the impression of being slightly "cold." They respected me but loved him. Together, we made a balanced team, complementing each other's strengths and weaknesses. His card-playing experience made him much more of a gambler; he was willing to take larger chances than my more conservative nature permitted me to consider.

Whether or not our birth order accounted for it, Eddie and I were decidedly different. That difference more often strengthened our contributions during our long years together as executives of Neiman Marcus.

November 26, 1991

Flowers Express Their Gratitude

Others before me have written thousands of paragraphs on the joys of gardening, and some of them I have read. Since I don't pretend to be an avid gardener, I haven't permitted myself to become immersed in horticultural literature.

Only recently, in Santa Fe, the title of "chief waterer" has been bestowed on me. Since I'm not considered knowledgeable enough to discriminate between a weed and a sprouting descia, my responsibilities are restricted to soaking the earth.

At first, I was a little miffed by this limitation, but I soon found that Emerson's Law of Compensation works on matters of flower cultivation as well as on more philosophical subjects.

Watering can be done with equal proficiency seated or standing, whereas gardening requires kneeling and squatting, both of which are tough on aging knees. An exercise program can be adopted by a water sprayer without wasting a single drop of water, for the motions of pulling a hose can serve to stretch back and abdominal muscles, arms and legs, neck and toes. This can be a solace to those who are jealous of their time.

A hose is not a lethal instrument that can turn around and bite or scar the user. You can get water in the eye but not on the knee. You can be far enough away from the pollen so you don't subject your nose and sinuses to the various allergic substances that are being exhaled by plants and bushes in full bloom—not to mention the hazards of bees and hummingbirds.

For both the health of the plants and the hose wielder, it is best to spray either early in the morning or just before dusk. The parching summer sun of Santa Fe is equal to that of Texas, and he who attempts to water after 9 o'clock in the morning must be unfamiliar with Noel Coward's song, "Mad dogs and Englishmen go out in the midday sun."

In most jobs, the result of efforts is seldom visible instantly, but watching a thirsty plant absorb and respond to water has some similarities to offering a full canteen to a parched hiker in the desert.

My mother, who was an inveterate gardener, startled me by her insistence that the flowers talked to her when she tended them. I think now that I understand what she meant, for I am getting a response, if not in words, from a wilted columbine or a drooping alyssum as I douse it with a shower of cold well water.

A lamb's ear perks itself and seems to look up in gratitude for the resuscitation. Many are the gifts I send that elicit a tardy response, but not so with my garden friends, who are both grateful and punctual in expressing their appreciation.

August 1, 1995

$\mathscr{G}$OOD GOVERNMENT

Governance Needs Openness

I recently reread *The Decision Makers/The Power Structure of Dallas*, a book written by Carol Estes Thometz and published by Southern Methodist University Press in 1963. I had read it when it was issued, but its contents had slipped my mind.

Commenting on a study of Dallas' power structure, Mrs. Thometz observed, "Recent events indicate that many of the conditions which existed at the time of the study are now in a state of flux. These changes appear to result from community growth, as well as state and local political developments. As Dallas continues to grow and become industrially and politically more complex, other forces will come into play which likewise will affect the distribution of power."

She also quoted a *Fortune* magazine article that described the city's leaders this way: "They run it well, with self-effacement, not for private gain."

Mrs. Thometz's forecast was accurate, for things have indeed changed. We now have a more democratically elected Dallas City Council, whose composition and competence should reflect in time a growing sophistication of the voters and their demand for council responsibility.

If the local electorate demonstrates the same type of awakening that occurred in the most recent congressional election, it will give more scrutiny to the quality of integrity, an ancient virtue that still is the most valuable attribute for not only elected officials but members of the municipal bureaucracy, too.

If our city manager form of government is to survive, we must have more openness at City Hall—not less—and more disclosure of details with regard to construction projects and their locations—not fewer.

There is always a reason to withhold information on negotiations, but good government for all of the people benefits from more daylight. It provides open answers rather than raises questions about the integrity of elected or appointed officials.

Integrity also applies to citizens doing business with the government. Dallas has had a happy history of civic leaders who contributed their time and efforts, with no consideration of personal financial benefits. It is a tradition that today's business leaders should find useful to study and emulate.

If a government loses its reputation for integrity, its bond issues will lose popularity. If citizens conduct deals with the government behind veils of secrecy, they are as guilty as corrupt officials.

Integrity is a two-way street.

January 24, 1995

Carrying a Grudge Is Poor Exercise

For the past few years, I have been conducting research on the status of grudges. I am referring not only to the deadly ones like the Hatfields and McCoys had but also to the less lethal ones that occur in business, the professions and family life.

Some years ago, I quoted a sign that I saw in Florence's famous Uffizi gallery, which read, "Please do not touch the paintings: First, it may damage the art; second, it's against the law; third, it is useless."

That same philosophy, I think, applies to grudges, for even if they aren't illegal, they will damage human relations and they are completely useless. Children shouldn't be permitted to develop grudges, and adults should have enough common sense to realize that nothing beneficial occurs to justify them.

The cultivation of grudges takes time and energy that would be better spent on something constructive like watering the grass or beating the rugs, as our grandparents used to do. Those substitutes distract your mind from real or fancied insults and release the tensions in your back and the sourness in your mouth.

Business and the professions are learning to use the techniques of mediation to resolve differences of opinions and thereby eliminating the necessity of going through the tribulations and costs of legal action. Each side agrees to accept the verdict of the mediator, who extracts a concession from one side and then one from the other, until both parties are softened up sufficiently to come to a compromise. After all, that is what life is all about.

In some instances, individuals are following the same trend in settling scores with those with whom they may have violent disagreements. In the past, grudges existed between siblings, between mothers-in-law and daughters-in-law and even between husbands and wives. My research shows that participants gradually are recognizing that family disputes are useless and needlessly destructive to family values. "Let's talk it out" is replacing the old doctrine of "Let's fight it out."

It isn't unusual for two people who come from different backgrounds to have their individual ideas on how to hold a steak knife or a demitasse cup, on who invites whom first or on when to send a thank-you note, but there is no use in carrying a grudge for such minor disagreements. If mothers-in-law and their daughters-in-law would discuss their different opinions on how to make their son and husband happy, I am confident they will enhance their own relationships and make their son or husband a much happier man.

About the only group that continues to hold grudges is drivers caught in heavy traffic. They show a tendency to avenge a perceived highway insult by pulling out a pistol or shotgun and settling the grudge then and there. That hardly is the solution you would expect from adults, who then spend the next ten years behind bars for manslaughter.

Life is just too short to spend fussing or in prison when the same amount of time can be put to constructive use. If you happen to know any individuals that this article characterizes, hand them copies of it for them to read.

December 31, 1996

Clean Desk or Messy, the Debate Rages On

In medieval times, the hot debate was how many angels could dance on the head of a pin. Today, an equally inexhaustible subject is the comparative virtues of a clean desk vs. a cluttered one. There seem to be two types of people: those whose desk tops are vast expanses of polished perfection, interrupted only by perfectly positioned accessories, and those whose work surfaces resemble the aftermath of a tornado at the city dump. There is apparently no median between the two extremes, and the proponents of each style consider theirs to be superior and look with disdain on those who hold the opposite persuasion.

Psychologists and behaviorists have analyzed the phenomenon, with little agreement. Some say the clean desk person is one who is well organized, efficient and on top of things, while the cluttered desk person lacks self-control, does inadequate work and is devoid of ambition. Others say a cluttered desk shows a creative, active mind, while a clean desk indicates compulsiveness and an absence of imagination. Further theories say the cluttered desk person is frustrated by his work, and the clean desk person has reached the pinnacle of his potential.

We've all known examples of all these types. I know a successful retail executive who defends his chaotic desk by saying that being surrounded by things stimulates his imagination. On the other hand, one of the most brilliant and innovative advertising executives I've met was a polished-desk type.

I am fascinated with those messy deskers who have the ability to extract any given letter from the midst of the litter.

61

I envy those who can keep an orderly desk. I've tried for years to discipline myself not to move a single paper until I find a permanent place for it, but something inevitably forces me to deviate from my resolve.

When we expect guests for a party, my wife gathers my litter and places it in shopping bags in an adjacent closet. Upon the guests' departure, the bags are returned to my desk for the contents to be relittered.

I'm fascinated by the theories but think the way a person arranges his work space has no more value in revealing his potential for success than does his liking or disliking of broccoli.

April 3, 1990

You Can't Always Catch Happiness

Abraham Lincoln was such a good penman of bits of wisdom that it wasn't often that he wrote something subject to change. But his observation that "most folks are about as happy as they make up their minds to be" deserves critical evaluation and shouldn't be swallowed in its raw state.

Some people face such difficult living conditions that they abandon hope early in the game. They may be anti-social and unwilling to exert themselves to be nice "unto others"—apparently not concerned that good deeds come back to the bestower. Happiness, like so many of life's attributes, requires effort. It provides an adhesive quality to the individual who tries.

Certainly, there are some who consciously adopt a happiness standard that suits them or that at least provides a platform where life can be tolerable, even if not thoroughly enjoyable. Those who have recurrent instances of hard luck—successive illnesses, brutality from a family member specifically or society in general, destruction of personal property by floods, hurricanes, earthquakes or other vagaries of nature—are very apt to have a sour taste about everything.

It is easier to smile when things are going your way—or at least not aimed at you. The face usually reflects an individual's state of being. People don't smile as much when they are in pain or when they lack the necessary payments on a car loan or a tuition fee. There are extreme examples of individuals who haven't smiled in years and aren't about to join in a general celebration of the joys of life or even an old-fashioned Irish stew. It is too bad that they fail to share grins. Their glumness often discourages invitations to participate in social functions.

While the Declaration of Independence doesn't guarantee the right to be happy, it states, "We hold these truths to be self-evident, that all men are created equal, that they are endowed by their creator with certain unalienable rights, that among these are life, liberty and the pursuit of happiness."

With good judgment, the scribes of the document left it to the individual to adopt the face and demeanor of his choosing. Just imagine: If the Declaration had been written to guarantee the right to happiness, we now would be surrounded by "happiness police" whose job was to enforce the anti-spoilsport law.

To set the record straight, the Declaration of Independence guaranteed the pursuit of happiness to every citizen of the new country—a subject that still is being argued about 200 years later. It sounds more like a hunting license than an assured right to pursue that effervescent and nebulous quality called "happiness."

Good hunting is the result of an optimistic frame of mind, strong family relations and good luck.

July 14, 1998

Please, Suffer in Silence

Rich and poor, young and old, wise and otherwise, the common cold strikes us all, and it turns the best of us into sneezing, sniveling complainers. Here are a few common-sense rules that may make the common cold more bearable.

At the risk of sounding cold-hearted, I think there's only one thing worse than having a cold. That's being around someone who has a cold, but there are some things we can all do to make our colds easier for the people around us to live with. First and foremost, we can avoid talking about our colds. With all your sniffling and sneezing and coughing, who could miss the fact that you have a cold?

In fact, a second suggestion is to avoid talking at all when you have a cold. It's often a strain. It's hard to be taken seriously when you sound like you're talking through your nose. Besides, every time you open your mouth, you spread thousands of germs.

It seems strange that the Western world has failed to follow the example of the Japanese, who wear gauze masks to prevent the dissemination of the cold germs. This is a practice that makes sense for individuals who perform intimate, personal services, as do dentists, beauticians and barbers. They should wear such masks on all such occasions, with or without a cold.

A third rule is one you've probably heard from your mother. Cover your mouth when you cough or sneeze, especially in meetings or on crowded buses. And, if your hands are full, ask the person next to you to hold your parcels. Only if he or she refuses is it considered proper to let them have it.

My fourth rule is for friends of the cold sufferer. The rule is:

Don't offer cold remedies—not your aunt's famous chicken soup, nor your uncle's hot toddy recipe, nor even those little tiny pills. After all, everyone knows there's no cure for the common cold as yet, so why give the cold sufferer hope when there is none?

The next time you have a cold, stay at home for a couple of days. An occasional day in bed is something we all need. You may not get over your cold any faster, but the rest may enable you to avoid complications and side effects. With any luck, your associates will avoid catching it at all.

This skepticism about the treatment of colds is based on experience over the years, during which I have seen and tried scores of new products advertised to cure, prevent, or alleviate this malady. Reluctantly, I have come to realize that a cold must take its natural course of one week or seven days, whichever is shorter.

September 11, 1990

For Long Life, Learn Rules of Good Health

It takes a lifetime, and a long one at that, to learn the importance of following the rules for good health.

The body gives off signals that must be classified according to their importance. Youths aren't prepared to receive and translate those warnings into action. And parents are apt either to ignore anything less than three degrees of fever or to overreact to the trivia of a seven-year-old child's self-established health bulletin.

As we grow up and survive the minor and traditional illnesses of childhood, we are inclined to pay scant attention to symptoms that older and experienced individuals would recognize as warnings worth continued observation.

If one is observant, it is fairly easy to figure out what food causes skin rashes and which exercises result in headaches or upset stomachs. That kind of information is helpful to a doctor trying to determine the cause of an ailment.

The fear of being labeled a hypochondriac discourages many children and adults from telling their physicians about a reaction to a certain food, the swelling of the lymphatic glands or a shortness of breath. Such vital subjects as posture and its effects on the mechanics of the body are given scant attention, which leads to malfunctions later in life.

Hygiene wasn't taught very well eighty years ago and, from what I hear, still isn't regarded as a course of primary importance, despite the fact that the subject is distinctly more important than almost anything that is in the curriculum. Personal health should be taught continuously until the completion of a student's education.

A healthy life requires a number of contributions from diverse people: (1) parents, who probably should be required to attend a course on children's health when their first child is born; (2) good schoolteachers, who indoctrinate children with basic health information; and (3) patient physicians, who have the time to listen.

This needs to be developed as a skillfully administered educational program so that children don't become overly conscious of every ache and pain that they then magnify. All of this sounds very complex, but so did Latin, geometry and space problems until we learned how to solve those problems.

Good health procedures range from tooth brushing to proper shoe fitting. Diet counseling should be taught in an innovative manner that will ensure a complete understanding of its vital importance. Too often this comes only at a stage in life when the damage done by a faulty diet is irreparable.

Health is such an obviously important subject to every person that the teaching of it should be given even higher ranking on the list of educational objectives.

July 15, 1997

Imagination Can Enliven a Strike

Surely there's nothing more upsetting than a strike, whether you're a participant walking a picket line or a tourist whose sightseeing routine is upset. But I heard of a strike not long ago of an entirely different flavor.

Italy is a place famous for its sunny climate, its ancient art treasures and its frequent strikes. When you do something often enough, you get good at it. Maybe that's why the Italians are bringing as much originality to their workers' protests as they do to the design of ceramics and men's fashions.

I was intrigued to hear of a waiters' strike in Italy. Diners were seated as usual, and their orders were courteously taken. Then they were served impeccably—except in reverse order. The startled diners found themselves starting with coffee and liqueurs, then working backward with dessert, entree, soup and finally the appetizers. Instead of soup to nuts, it was spumoni to antipasto.

My source didn't tell me how the diners reacted to this version of Alice-in-Wonderland dining, but if I had been management, I would have been so delighted with this different type of strike that I probably would have met the waiters' demands.

Wouldn't life be a lot more interesting if management issued invitations for conciliation rather than mandates of toughness, and if all workers presented protests that went beyond the picket line? Striking bus drivers could take us on drives in the country. Newspaper pressmen could present us with novels or whodunits instead of the news. Coal strikers might give us guided tours of the mine. Or, perhaps, if unions put some real thinking into the problem, maybe they could start negotiating with management on its own level. They could divert some of the strike emergency funds, assign each member a manager to take a few hours off in the middle of the day, and take a boss to a one-on-one bargaining table over a three-martini lunch!

One of the most civilized strikes I ever witnessed was in Japan, where workers wore white head bands imprinted in black and red with the Japanese word for "protest" to indicate they were striking. The workers continued with their jobs, but at the morning break and again at lunchtime, they conducted peaceful mass protests and reiterated their complaints.

By the next morning, the work protest had been dealt with by an enlightened management and a worker strike team. Grievances were settled; neither side claimed victory, nor was the public egregiously inconvenienced. That always impressed me as a civilized way of settling a dispute.

Perhaps more problems between labor and management could be solved without resorting to the same old predictable, unproductive strikes if both sides would demonstrate the same kind of creative thinking as the Italian waiters.

August 4, 1992

Once Upon a Time, Wristwatches Were Rare

In the summertime, when short-sleeved sport shirts are the order of the day, wristwatches worn by men are more conspicuous than in the winter months, when long-sleeved shirts and coat jackets tend to mask them.

I pointed this out to a friend at a ballgame, which led him to ask about the origin of this fashion. I had some hazy idea that wristwatches had first appeared during World War I, but I wasn't positive.

A little research in *The History of Clocks and Watches* proved my recollection to be partly correct. A bracelet watch was made for the Empress Josephine, the wife of Napoleon, in the early 1800s. A duplicate bracelet was made by a jeweler named Nitot in Paris in 1806, which the empress presented, along with her own wristwatch, to her daughter-in-law, Princess Amalie Augusta, on the occasion of her marriage the following year.

Apparently the first use of the wristwatch by males occurred in 1880, when German naval officers bought quite small wristwatches, one inch in diameter, from a well-known watchmaker in Switzerland, Girard-Perregaux.

An effort to sell them to the public was unsuccessful, and it was not until the next century when artillery officers thought they would be much more practical than having to pick out a pocket watch every time a command was fired. The first of these watches were like small pocket watches held in leather cups on wrist straps.

During World War I, Dallas was flooded by cadet aviators who were being taught how to fly aeroplanes at Love Field. Young men from all parts of the country and from England spent hot summer months earning their gold bars as second lieutenants.

I made friends with some of these glamorous young men (in the eyes of a 13-year-old boy) and remember seeing my first wristwatch on the wrists of some of the student pilots. I wanted to wear one, but my fellow students at John Henry Brown grammar school derided the idea as being a "sissy affectation."

It wasn't until about 1918 that the wristwatch became ubiquitous enough to eliminate any such association.

The wristwatch went through a series of generational changes, including the invention of a quartz battery that eliminated the need for a nocturnal winding.

Once the popularity of wristwatches occurred, the pocket watch was virtually driven off the marketplace, much like the effect of the automobile on the horse and wagon. Henry Ford's mass-produced automobile swept away the last holdout, much as the machine-made Ingersoll watch finished off the gold pocket watch.

August 29, 1995

❧

Fax Revolutionizes Society

The introduction of the facsimile machine has revolutionized communications.

The "fax," as it is familiarly called, provides an alternative to overnight express mail or the telegram, which has all but disappeared from general usage.

It saves days of delivery time to foreign countries that have lethargic delivery schedules, speeding up the transmission of business information.

What's more, personal letters can be sent via fax so that familial correspondence can retain most of the characteristics of a handwritten letter.

Many entities that formerly required original signatures on contracts, income taxes, sales agreements and wills now are willing to accept those sent by fax. A sender can request verification by a return message if there is any skepticism that it may not have been received. Those who receive a large volume of faxes have found it worthwhile to use colored paper for incoming messages to differentiate them from other paper piled on a desk.

One unforeseen problem recently has come into focus and cries for correction: Most letterheads carry phone and fax numbers in very small type at the bottom of the page. Often, the end of a page doesn't get printed as clearly as the body of a message, and even when it does get printed, the small 6s, 8s and 0s tend to be filled in by ink and become distorted. Fax users have found that the nonreceipt of a message often is due to the 6s looking like 8s or 0s.

The solution, of course, is to design letterheads with larger numbers and preferably at the top of the page. This may prove to be a bonanza for the printing trade.

As another example of changed needs, laptop computers require a padded carrying case to protect the instruments from being battered as they are toted across the country by their owners. This should become a star gift for both women and men by next Christmas.

And, of course, home computers have created a need for a vast number of new supporting products—from furniture to armrests to foot stands.

One thing invariably leads to another.

February 13, 1996

Innovations Should Be Matched with a Respect for the Past

Innovation in cooking is as important to the vitality of that craft as innovation is to experimental architecture, painting or fashion. New solutions and methods emerge from trying different ways of renovating old forms.

I am most enthusiastic about such experimentation, but I find myself wishing that chefs, dress designers and architects were not so arrogant as to "cast off" the past in some sort of disdain without paying some respect to that which went before. Some recognition should be given to the milestones of discovery that make the present possible in any field of expression.

L'Exhibition des Arts Decoratif opened in 1925, and I had the good fortune to be there on my initial trip to Paris. It opened my eyes and pushed me urgently in the direction of contemporary design in architecture, art and design in general.

There were compelling reasons for architects to design buildings in the contemporary idiom. The industrial revolution in the 19th century had introduced mass production, which in itself anticipated and made uneconomical, centuries-old methods of construction antiquated. This exhibition introduced new concepts of design which further propelled the architecture and furniture designs into the 20th century.

Painters and sculptors were impressed by the new architectural forms and they responded with art that fitted into the new environments. Some even took the liberty of recreating man into abstract shapes or into forms that at first seemed grotesque, until we learned to read the new vocabulary.

Fashion designers were slow to catch the importance of the new revolution in production. It wasn't until about 1950 that they began to question the age-old techniques of making garments. Metal grippers used in cowboy shirts made more sense than closing a shirt front with buttons and button holes, but the public turned them down for general usage. On the other hand, an even more

74

radical invention, the zipper, was accepted relatively quickly by male and female customers who found them easier to use and in some cases even decorative.

Fabric fusing instead of sewing is still a long way off from meeting designer and customer acceptance. But in the need for economy in production, some form of it will overcome public inertia.

There is a temptation for many creative artists to glorify themselves in the act of leading a revolution. Many of them get carried away by public recognition, and they find themselves in the midst of a huge ego trip that leads them to forget that their mission is to design for human beings and to make their habitats more pleasant, more affordable, and their clothes more flattering and comfortable.

This syndrome happens to sports idols, actors and actresses, and even sports franchise owners who lose touch with reality and begin to inhale their own publicity until they convince themselves that they are "above the law."

Now back to the opening paragraph of this piece, which started with the innovation in cooking called *nouvelle cuisine*. Often a chef can become so concentrated on developing new flavors and presentations that he forgets that many of his customers who are enthusiastically enjoying an occasional dish of mango juice with crushed anchovy and a dash of cumin as a sea for two shrimp are still longing for some comfortable old-fashioned dishes that are being neglected, such as an Irish lamb stew, pot roast, baked chicken, a French *daube* or boiled beef. Chefs should continue to offer innovations, but they should throw in one "standard" as they used to say in dance band circles.

Too frequently, chefs become concerned with the design of the food on the plate and forget that the taste is what makes the eaters ask for seconds. The same condition exists in music, as Olin Chism, staff critic of this newspaper, noted recently in a review of 20th-century music. As he wrote, "the proponents of atonality failed where any revolution must succeed. They lost the hearts and minds of listeners."

July 30, 1996

The Invention That Changed Texas

The fact that this has been designated "National Engineers Week" brings to mind one of the most important engineering achievements of the century—the invention and marketing of air conditioning equipment.

The 20th century has been full of discoveries and inventions, all of which have revolutionized our way of life and the economies of the world. But none has affected human comfort more than air conditioning.

As a resident of Texas since 1905, I grew up in the days when the only relief from the blistering hot summer nights was the screened porch with its overhead fan. Directing fans over blocks of ice gave succor to anyone within two feet but no farther. Other cooling aids were ice-cold watermelon, ice-cold lemonade and electric fans blowing across water-soaked bedsheets.

Otherwise, it was just plain misery. Going to a movie to cool off wasn't possible, because the movies were shown in open-air theaters.

Experiments in the development of cooling devices had been going on for fifty or more years, but it was Willis H. Carrier who invented the most practical device in 1902.

With the installation of the first air-cooling units, it was possible to cool off in enclosed movie theaters, to ride a train without the ever-present soot from outside, to read a newspaper or book without being bothered by the myriad insects that penetrated even the finest window screens, to sleep in comfort on days when the outside temperature was over 100, to attend an indoor religious service or a summer school class, to eat in a dining room and to avoid chigger-infested lawns.

Those benefits and many others were enjoyed by all ages. Summer in Texas became tolerable—if not enjoyable.

In Texas and other cotton-growing states, the cotton-picking season ran from mid-July to mid-August. That necessitated all cotton-related executives to be in their offices during those critical days.

If the boll weevils hadn't gotten into the cotton and if the rains had occurred at the proper moment in the growth cycle, there would be a large crop. That required additional pickers to pick and handle the crop, which meant higher wages.

Most of the money so earned went to the doctors, lawyers, druggists and grocers who had financed growers over the long winter. When they got paid, they in turn retired their bank loans. Everybody made money, and there was general prosperity.

Thus, it was important for the business leaders in cotton-growing areas to be in town in midsummer. Because of the oppressive heat, they sent their wives and children to Colorado or the Ozarks to cool off. Meanwhile, the male fold, forced to stay behind for four to six weeks alone, frequently got into trouble.

When the arrival of air conditioning made it comfortable enough for wives to stay in town over the summer, the whole moral climate was cured. That was one of the least reported but most important benefits of Mr. Carrier's little invention.

February 24, 1998

OBS

Getting Noticed to Get the Job

As the job market grows more competitive, people are being forced to seek more than just work—they're having to look for innovative ways to get that work.

Job hunters are finding times to be more competitive than ever, and though most people have yet to give up on the traditional employment tactics, some are finding that unusual methods can sometimes help them get their feet in the door.

The *Wall Street Journal* told of a good example. She is Jo Mapes, and she was laid off after fifteen years as an advertising copy writer, but Jo refused to take her layoff lying down. She put her ample creative skills back to work—this time for herself. Jo wrote her resume on a sandwich board and took to the streets of Chicago. Her inventiveness paid off. She got a job.

According to most career counselors, off-beat job search tactics are more often off target. Still, you can't argue with the fact that the unusual gets attention. Lots of job hunters are finding that it's not bad to be creative, especially when you're looking for a creative job—like the Cornell grad who snagged a reporting position by writing her resume as a mock front page—or the woman who landed a job in publishing by binding her resume in a small, hardcover book.

Some professions, though, aren't as likely to appreciate the innovative job seeker. For instance, the accountant who sends his resume out on a starched, white, button-down shirt will probably not be taken seriously. And in a profession like accounting, an earnest image is all important. So how do you know when to be daring?

One angle that seems to escape most job seekers is a clear statement as to what profitable contribution the "j.s." could make to the prospective employer.

Most companies are impressed by an applicant who can present a convincing plan to attract more business. Most law firms would welcome a lawyer who can bring in new clients. There is hardly a baseball team that wouldn't respond favorably to a .345 hitter. Almost all retail stores will welcome an experienced salesperson with a large clientele.

All of these suggestions require the applicant to think out the unique selling proposition that would arouse a favorable response to a need. Nobody has ever said that this approach is easy, but it has worked successfully.

One general rule all job hunters might find helpful: Don't go overboard with innovative job search methods. Remember, inventiveness is a combination of brains and materials—the more brains you have, the fewer materials you need.

June 2, 1992

ISSING

The Reducing Power of Love

Obesity may be hereditary, or it may be due to an imbalanced glandular system, or it may result from a plain lack of willpower. The doctors render a little aid to the first two categories, but to the third they simply pass out the advice, "stop eating" as if those overweight souls don't know they should do that already.

The obese, or let's call them what they are—"the fat ones"—dream of two things night in and night out. They dream of mounds of mouth-watering foods of which they are guiltily partaking, and they dream of losing ten pounds overnight without the effort of exercise or the restrictions of a diet.

On arising, they first look at their stomachs, and when they find them the same size as at bedtime, they resolve this day they are really going to start a serious diet—a resolution that lasts until breakfast.

The plump are tired of being overweight. That's why they are such suckers for newspaper and magazine advertisements that herald "the new secret diet used by the stars."

Normal exercise doesn't evaporate an ounce, and only tortuous jogging plus radically controlled rations will take off a pound a week. Fifty pounds of overweight can be eliminated in fifty weeks, provided there's not a moment of backsliding.

But now comes a new diet that has much to recommend it, for it promises to be fun as well as effective.

Even love has its price in an age when the energy conscious are counting up the cost of everything from gasoline to a kiss. Italian nutritionists, armed with a computer, have calculated the energy cost of a kiss varies between six and twelve calories.

According to an article in *The Environmental Nutrition Newsletter*, it all depends on the power of your pucker. A round of lovemaking can burn up as many as 300 calories, or as few as 125. The key is intensity—the basis of energy expenditure. Important variables include ambiance and technique, but you'll have to talk to your coach about those.

On an annual basis, three kisses a day at an average cost of nine calories add up to a 52-week tab of 9,855 calories. Two amorous interludes a week at 212.5 calories per episode work out to 22,100 calories over a full year. The grand total for kissing and lovemaking on that schedule is 31,955 calories of energy consumption in twelve months.

Since a hard-boiled egg has a value of 50 calories, then those 31,955 calories equate to 639 eggs. During an amorous courtship, complete with steak dinners and champagne breakfasts, one might end up just breaking even. But, either way, you can't lose—so to speak.

If you choose the kissing diet as a regular program of weight reduction, you can expect to lose 9.13 pounds in a year's time. If you want to lose more, just step up your kissing program, or speed up your K.P.M. And, even if you don't lose any weight at all, at least you had a good time trying!

February 12, 1985

Animals Dominate Our Language

Medieval calligraphers on up to contemporary book printers have enjoyed the typographical exercise of creating books with animal illustrations. Occasionally, the animals, twenty-six in number, were related to the letters of the alphabet, viz, *C* as in cat, *D* as in dog, etc. Such books carry the name "bestiaries."

Although I've been using the English language, for better or worse, during 80 of my 82 years, I had not realized how much our vocabulary has drawn upon the names of animals, fowl and insects to enrich the imagery of our conversations.

We use these words daily and so frequently that we become totally unaware of our practice. If, for example, we want to express complete exhaustion, we say "dog tired," or if we choose to describe a well-used book, we refer to it as "dogeared." Golf players usually bemoan a "dogleg" hole. Hot weather means "the dog days," and a man of my age might be referred to as "a gay old dog," long past the state of "puppy love."

If we have a "black sheep" in the family, we refer to him as "gone to the dogs," but if he doesn't cause us too much trouble, we might tend to ignore him with the explanation of "let sleeping dogs lie." We have "hawks" and "doves," both of which can be "mulish" in their attitudes. As long as they don't make "asses" of themselves, we can tolerate them. If we want to buy an impressive gift for a loved one, we might buy a "cat's-eye" ring or we might just send some "tiger lilies."

We use animals' and fowls' names, not only as adjectives like "catty," "kittenish," "bullish," and "bearish," but also as plain verbs such as "rat on a friend," "hog the spotlight," "cow a witness," and "goose a companion."

We use them as standards of comparison, such as "slippery as an eel," "proud as a peacock," "sly as a fox," "wise as an owl," "meek as a lamb," "stubborn as a mule," "strong as an ox" and "crooked as a snake." If we play our gin game "doggedly," we can avoid being "skunked." But experienced gamblers avoid "card sharks," unless they're carrying a "rabbit's foot."

We describe a teen-ager as having a "ducktail," a chief executive as being "top dog," intemperate men as "wild bulls," a Lothario as a "tomcat," a pallid lass as "mousy," a second-term president as a "lame duck," a lone sentry as a "sitting duck," an unattractive child as an "ugly duckling" and a marital ex as a "louse."

Our hitless ball team scores a "goose egg" because one of the players "loused up a throw to first." In such a case, runs are "scarce as hens' teeth." If we "smell a rat," we're apt to "let the cat out of the bag." If we are terrifically hungry, we can become "pigs" as we "wolf" down a meal.

The news editor waits for the "bulldog edition" before he "bulldozes" the front page. We beware of "quacks," but when we like something, we might call it the "cat's meow." That is better than being referred to as a "cat's-paw."

If we don't "chicken" out in life, there's always the chance we might end up being "top dog." Much as man esteems his best friend, the dog, he labels a bad-selling article derogatively as a "dog," and if he's a theatrical producer, he prefers to eat a chicken sandwich, for a "turkey" is a synonym for a complete flop. People who "ape" or "parrot" others gain the reputation of being "copycats." A good way to avoid that epithet is to sit "catercorner" with your back to the simian and polly.

When we go to the flicks to see a "horse opera," we don't "put on the dog." Instead, we don a pair of slacks and a "houndstooth" patterned jacket. If a judge hears completely fresh evidence, he might well comment, "That's a horse of a different color."

We place a bet or buy a stock when we get a tip "right out of the horse's mouth." We used to "walk a mile for a Camel," unless we were suffering from a "charley horse." When we need a mild expletive, we say, "Doggone it."

If I had any "horse sense," I'd go "bell the cat"; I should "duck out" and quit "horsing around."

"Horsefeathers" or "rats"—as the case may be—if I don't feel better in the morning, I'll take a shot of the "hair of the dog that bit me."

May 26, 1987

≥❧

Language Reveals Age

It's not only the facial wrinkles or the slackening gait that forecasts the aging process. Memories become hazy, and vision dims; simultaneously, appetites fade, and nostalgia tends to supplant reality.

Less obvious is the use of words which were once a part of one's daily vocabulary that are now outdated and used infrequently. When, by chance, such a word creeps into a conversation with a younger person, communication ceases, for the listener finds it to be unintelligible, as though it were of Sanskrit origin.

I find myself to be guilty of using such out-of-date words when occasionally they slip into my conversation. The other night I was conversing with my 25-year-old granddaughter about a decorative object, and I referred to it as "an old chromo." "What did you say?" she inquired. "An old chromo," was my reply.

The puzzled look on her face forced me to reconsider my remark, and I quickly recognized that I had used a word belonging to a 1925 conversation instead of 1995. "Chromo" is a construction of the word "chromolithograph," a color printing process that was in great favor in the early part of this century. Chromolithographs were polychromatic to the extreme and tended to be garish and overcolored. Hence, the word "chromo" from the Greek "chromos"

85

was the contraction I used to deprecate a gaudy or overdecorated object.

Another word in disuse today is "borax." It is defined as "cheaply made from inferior materials; a gaudy article showing bad taste." Around 1920, a merchant might refer to a piece of merchandise as being "pure borax," and his associates would understand him exactly. Today, a 50-year-old person would have no comprehension of the term.

Similarly, I have referred to a record player as a "Victrola," a trademarked name for such instruments of the 1910-20 vintage. No current teenager would have a clue as to what I meant.

I was discussing vintage-word problems with a friend, who said he was talking to his 35-year-old daughter and his 10-year-old grandson and was describing the forces of change that are so prevalent today. He said, "For example, the Sun 490 looks like an icebox." His daughter interrupted to say, "I don't know what you are talking about. What is a Sun 490?" The grandson immediately chimed in and asked, "What is an icebox?"

This is what is known as a generation gap.

May 16, 1995

❧

Our Insincere Greetings

Many observers have commented that the art of letter writing has been virtually destroyed by long-distance phone service. Others might add that the art of conversation has been reduced by the ever present television, which intrudes itself on verbal communication.

Upon greeting another person, the common salutation is "Hi!" which takes a split second to get off. The response is likely to be "OK," which takes slightly longer.

A lengthy discussion may be amplified by "How're things?" or "How're you doing?"—questions to which answers are not really expected. The best reply to the latter was one a hotel doorman used. "Not as well as you're doing, or as well as I'd like to be doing." Certainly, no one really wants a descriptive answer to a rhetorical question such as "How are you?" or a detailed listing of aches and pains, stomach rumblings and sleepless nights. A listener does not expect an answer nor really want one.

Every language develops its own shorthand salutations, but most are expressed with more feeling and verve, as when a Frenchman sees an acquaintance and says, "Bon jour, mon ami," or "Comment-allez vous?" Even a German's "Guten Tag" is delivered with the importance of an assertion rather than as a mere weather report. A vigorous "Good morning" or "Good evening" is a highly recommended greeting.

At least these are better than the advice, "Have a nice day," which has always seemed to me to be a clumsy attempt to become overly familiar. As I wrote some years ago, I try to discourage such inanities by replying, "I can't. I've made other plans."

Another bromide that has developed currency in the past few years is an expression used after one has thanked a person for a kindness or favor. More likely than not, you will get the reply, "It's my pleasure," which to my ear sounds pompous and insincere compared with the simpler, "It was nothing" or "You are welcome." It's gratifying that the most painful stereotypical greeting of all time, "Long time no see," has practically disappeared from daily usage.

One of the advantages of carrying a cane is that it provides you with a ready instrument to poke such verbal libertines in the ribs. June 20, 1995

We Should Spring Clean Our Vocabularies

Very shortly, industrious homeowners will be getting their houses ready for spring cleaning. But as conscious as we are of the need to clean our homes, we give little thought to periodically cleaning up our vocabularies of outdated phrases.

I recently have been recording, in my little black book, fragments of speech not only from my friends' conversations, but from my own as well. I have been impressed by the amount of verbiage with which we indulge ourselves—cases where we repeat grammatical structures that add very little to our conversations and actually impede the clarity of our communications.

Here are some examples I have pulled from my notebook:

• "*Would you mind* passing the water?" Why not just say, "Please pass the water"? The italicized words are a complete waste of time, for even if the person to whom we are talking did mind, she wouldn't say so.

• Another bit of circumlocution occurs when we say, "*I wonder* if you would open the door." That isn't a subject of wonderment at all. There is no mystery about opening a door; the person to whom you are talking may wonder why you are wondering enough to incorporate that word in your query.

• "It would be *nice* of you to close the door when you leave." That is a lot of bunk. Niceness has nothing to do with your willingness to close the door.

• "Will you be *nice* enough to help me on with my coat?" That request would make more sense by saying, "Please help me put on my coat." That gets the job done politely without getting the other party mixed up with your syntax.

• I have heard individuals say, "*Would it be possible* for you to lend me a hand with this job?" Of course, anything is possible, even though it may be *improbable*. "I would appreciate it if you would help me," would take less time to say and comes to the point. Both the speaker and listener would save time.

• Then there are a whole group of phrases used so repetitively that the listener usually blocks them out of his mind. They include: "Have a good day," "How ya doin?," "Long time no see," and "How do you do?" which is an approximate translation from the French phrase, "Comment allez vous?" As a test, I once tried to answer that question after three individuals greeted me with it. They each walked away. Having asked the question, they had no interest in the answer.

• Closely akin to those bromidic questions is, *"How would you like* to refill my coffee cup?" That is a mushy way for asking a favor. What if the person to whom the request was addressed would reply, "Certainly not! I wouldn't like to a bit"? The simple way of making such a request would have been, "Will you, please, refill my coffee cup?"

Yes, spring is a good time to clean up our verbiage as well as our closets.

February 10, 1998

ॐ

Mrs. Malaprop's Descendants Flourish

Ace Dallas printer Win Padgett, recalling my defense of the English language, brought me a booklet of malapropisms gathered by his friend Jack Goodrich, who had been an editor and typographer at a Dallas typesetting shop. In addition to being a good craftsman whose keen eyes found typographical errors, Mr. Goodrich's good ears caught these misuses of the English language.

Malapropisms are named for a character (Mrs. Malaprop) in Richard Sheridan's 18th-century comedy, *The Rival*. Today, people are more likely to remember her amusing and ludicrous use of words than Mr. Sheridan's play.

In the course of his thirty-year career with Southwestern Typographers, Mr. Goodrich picked up and recorded these malapropisms from customers and associates:

The doctor gave me a *subscription*.

The *maskhead* of the magazine.

"Are you a *connoisseur*? My shoulder needs to be massaged."

There is too much *distension* among the employees.

This job will have *inferior* and *exferior* figures.

The golf course was *immaculous*.

A *hole* life insurance policy.

Let's *redouble check* that.

Put in *numrical* order.

The most sloppiest work I have ever seen.

He agreed to *delinquish* his place on the vacation schedule.

We need some *incentative* to accomplish that.

We will see if this suits their satisfaction.

He *implicated* that he would send the job to us.

We will have to *reduplicate* that job.

That will *entrail* extra work.

We found a word that was misspelled wrong.

Everyone was in complete *agreeance*.

This will be almost virtually the same size.

Ron works *fluently* with me.

The doves were flying over *in pairs* of two, four and six.

We were *conferencing* about that.

That is one of his *downfaults*.

They were very *pacific* about that.

We are the most leading company in the business.

Let's be *consecutive* with the style. (Consistent)

It is the *ultrament* in design.

She was *misconceived* about this.

He gave a *disposition* in court.

We are going to run three jobs in *collusion*. (Succession)

We will have to tell him *intangibly* how it is to be done.
    (Emphatically)

I like him because he is always so *reluctant* to help. (Willing)

This is very *indifferent* from the one we used to have.

He just graduated from dental school and will take his bar exam
    next week.

It must be *presizely* 10 inches.

The outcome didn't come out like we wanted it to.

While education has reduced the number of Mrs. Malaprops and her unwitting verbal blunders, today's poor-spelling high school students still are providing many malapropisms.

March 10, 1998

ૐ

Where Are the Language Police?

Buildings deteriorate unless they get the benefit of a constant maintenance program. Human beings need increased maintenance and repair work as they age. And all language falls into disrepair unless people keep tabs on the verbal and written abuse they encounter.

As Pogo of cartoon fame once observed, "The enemy: he is us." We are the ones who ignore grammatical rules and accept flip pieces of slang into everyday speech without a protest. Not long ago, I wrote a column on the three-letter word "wow" that threatens to pollute our language as surely as gasoline fumes destroy fresh air.

I have no formal system to grade a column's popularity, but the number of casual comments, written or spoken, give a fair indication of its impact. The response to that particular column led me to rate it as one of the more popular I have written.

Young people from 5 to 25 have developed the habit of condensing their emotions of surprise, indignation, delight, disapproval and wonderment into one convenient, all-purpose word, "wow." This piece of verbal shorthand has proved to be so contagious that even Mom and Pop have become addicted, too.

Now, there is another all-purpose expression that ignores age and social rank and is even more dangerous than "wow." It is the use of "you guys" as a replacement for "Mr." or "Mrs.," "Sir" or

"Ma'am." It is easy to trace its origin, for it emanates from the gang world of *Guys and Dolls*. It has become a convenient way for a young waiter to address unknown guests at a restaurant or for a flight attendant to talk to a couple (defying most airlines' instructions to address passengers by their names preceded by Mr. or Mrs.)

"Guy" is showing up in print in all sorts of publications, even as it is emerging from the tongues of all sorts of people. On one day two weeks ago, you would have found "guy" in Maryln Schwartz's column, a *New York Times* editorial and a front-page news story. It is all over the place. Sooner or later, it will become a cliché, like "you all."

All of this has been bothering me for some time, but I am not the only one to feel this way. A reader, John Kohler, recently wrote me a letter expressing his apprehension of "these days when even girls are called guys" and his concern about the future when letters addressed to him will arrive without the "Mr."

France is the only nation that patrols the corruption of its language with diligence. To my knowledge, there is no official or self-appointed authority of like nature in this country. It would be wonderful if the chief executive officers of large organizations would spot-check outgoing mail to determine whether the proper protocol is being followed in the addressing of envelopes. It would help employees know that their bosses care about how the recipients of corporate mail are addressed.

March 17, 1998

Management Excellence Is No Mystery

What makes a good manager? Consistent productivity, long hours on the job, never making mistakes? Actually, none of these, according to a study reported some time ago in the *Wall Street Journal*.

Whether your territory is General Motors, the local fast-food franchise or the family business, if you manage it well, you're likely to have six traits, according to Charles Garfield, president of a human research firm.

You'll always be surpassing your previous performance; you don't get entrenched where you are; you enjoy your work as a kind of art form; you don't try to place blame when things go wrong; you examine risk before you commit yourself; and you rehearse coming events in your mind.

These characteristics describe a likable person, not a stick-in-the-mud, but the type who can challenge others without putting them down if their reach sometimes exceeds their grasp. To be a great boss, you must be relaxed and confident enough to allow both you and your employees to make occasional mistakes. There's no better way to stifle creativity than to terrorize those who sometimes fall by holding a kangaroo court to single out the guilty party.

If you're a good manager, you must have a lively imagination, and never be too busy to use it. Events go your way more often than not, because you've gone over all the contingencies in your mind, rehearsing your various responses to different cases. And if you're executive suite potential, there's one more trait that's useful—knowing the difference between a minor problem and a crisis.

Every successful business must deliver customer satisfaction, and that comes about only when the merchandise or service meets or excels the customer's anticipations.

What Mr. Garfield doesn't emphasize is the importance of common sense. American Airlines did pay full tribute to that quality when it authorized its supervisory staff to deviate from SOP (standard operating procedure) when those rules failed to provide passengers with satisfaction, and instead to go by the principles set forth in a new document, SIP (service improvement program), which assures staff members that they will not be reprimanded by breaking the rules to satisfy the traveler.

In my opinion, that has been one of the major breakthroughs in modern industrial management. Other companies have flirted with the idea, but I am unaware of any that stated this emancipation declaration more clearly and cogently than American Airlines.

Good management is common sense. It is based on Mr. Garfield's principles as well as on the Golden Rule.

July 31, 1990

ટ&

When Meetings Replace Work

A news item has come to my attention that says the average white-collar worker spends only 29 percent of his time working. The other 71 percent is spent attending meetings, searching for information and waiting for reports.

This statistic, if accurate, is somewhat shocking. If so much more time goes into planning work rather than actually doing it, how can one expect to maintain or increase productivity?

One of the major time-wasters in the white-collar world is the meeting. Properly done, meetings are vital and irreplaceable communication tools.

One of the techniques I used with success while a merchant

was the "morning meeting." Everyone from the chief executive to the stockroom clerk was made aware of the new fashion trends and merchandise arrivals in every department. This information made us all more effective in serving our customers.

Yet we all have sat through meetings, whether in our business, club or civic organization, that were more helpful for inducing sleep than anything else.

To keep meetings under control, I offer three suggestions: (1) Prepare an agenda in advance, stick to it, and don't permit others to deviate from it. (2) Have a time limit that is known to all participants; when the time is up, the meeting is over. (3) Select a moderator who is forceful yet tactful enough to enforce the first two rules.

One of the most successful devices I have found for keeping a meeting centered on the subjects listed on the agenda is to announce the time limit of the meeting in advance. That works wonders. I believe decisions for 90 percent of the subjects in meetings can be made within one hour of concentrated thinking and discussion.

Running a productive meeting requires great skill on the part of the chairperson, for feelings can be offended very easily if there is any indication that individuals are being ignored or their contributions are unappreciated.

I have commented on only one of the time-wasters cited in the study, but if you are one who spends more time meeting than working, I would advise you to look for another job. I don't think your management has the ability to survive hard times.

November 8, 1994

Casual Attitudes Affect More Than Dress

The trend toward casualization of attire has been commented on by both the printed and electronic press. On Fridays, offices across the country often resemble backyard barbecues so much that it wouldn't be surprising if an executive vice president asked the fellow in dirty jeans to pass him the catsup when he really meant to request the price quote that had just come in over the fax.

It is easy to attribute an explanation of this "dress down" trend to those manufacturers and retailers who have a poor clothing business and wanted the "go casual" movement to stimulate their less costly casual clothes.

That explanation was my first impulse, but several corollary movements tend to confirm that there is something in the air, the water, or in the bread that is encouraging similar casualization trends to take hold.

One illustration is in E-mail, which I discovered in my effort to master the arcane intricacies of the computer. I was in the process of writing an E-mail message to my granddaughter in Fort Worth. When I had finished it, I proceeded to correct some misspelled words, accidental use of lowercase instead of caps, and errant commas. But my guru turned to me and said, "E-mail, nobody bothers with corrections—everybody understands, for that's the way they write." Will this casual attitude toward writing correctness lead to the deterioration of our written word? This is a question well worth pondering.

A few days later, I came across a feature article in the *New York Times* on the subject of current accounting practices. Examples were given of executives of large companies who are pressing the accounting industry to adopt a more casual interpretation of accounting practices than was previously considered proper.

This trend is attributed in part to the fact that quarterly earnings reports required by the Securities and Exchange Commission act as an unintended pressure for chief executive officers to fudge their results by several devices to protect their stock prices. This, of course, is not the way accounting was taught at the Harvard Business School in 1925, or probably even today.

Such procedures led the SEC to accuse companies of "improper accounting." Other techniques for juggling results include the manner in which depreciation is charged leading to the overstatement of after-tax earnings.

John W. Baleen of Massachusetts Financial Services was quoted as saying, "Virtually every company has some element of aggressive accounting to it." Amy P. Sweeney, a Harvard Business School professor, commented, "Managers start out optimistic, they aren't quite getting the earnings, so they start to stretch a little. That kind of stretching never shows up if they're growing."

These attempts to stretch the truth are exactly why accounting rules have been very strict and even why the SEC was created—to protect the innocent purchasers of securities, the confident trading of which is the basis of our whole financial system. Accounting rules were established to protect the public from deception that can result from less rigid procedures.

We may be able to laugh off casual Friday's faded jeans and E-mail spelling, but there are very few stock owners who would vote for casualized accounting systems.

July 23, 1996

The Guardians of Manners

One of my recent columns on the subject of thank-you notes produced an unusual number of thank-you notes from readers.

No one took exception to the chidings I directed to those silent, unresponsive gift recipients who are either lazy, rude or ill-mannered. Most of the respondents made reference to early tutelage in the subject by their grandmothers. Note that the word is *grandmothers* and not *mothers*. Since I received almost a hundred letters, I decided to analyze this grandmother/mother distinction carefully.

It may suggest that grandmothers were more arduous in their efforts to educate the young about good manners than were their daughters. Or, it may signify that the social graces have been denigrated by contemporary mothers, or it may indicate that they have given up the task as being unimportant or irrelevant to the times.

In the case of broken families, a parent may have traumatized children and for that reason may hesitate to teach and enforce rules of conduct. A working mother has less time in which to educate her young and may be more likely to direct instruction to classroom subjects than to drawing room manners. Children in one-parent situations may not be given the kind of direction on the social obligations that are part of becoming responsible members of society.

It's not only gifts and acts of kindness that require acknowledgment, but many other manifestations of politeness to be observed. I'm thinking of prompt responses to invitations, remembrance of birthdays and other important events, visits to hospitalized associates, house calls to bereaved friends and cancellation of previously accepted invitations. These are not affectations to be ignored by this or any generation; they are simply niceties of conduct that distinguish us from other animals.

In former times, females lived in closer proximity to each other and had more intimate ties. The 20th-century search for greater independence ruptured the transmission of century-old customs and traditions. Contemporary generations wanted new freedoms; they got them. In the process of emptying the bath water, the baby has been thrown out as well. A society that ignores good manners simply elects to deal with its fellow members with indifference.

Since grandparents were so influential in previous generations, perhaps those of us in that category need to exercise our latent prerogatives of giving assistance to tired and discouraged parents. In cultures with more deeply rooted standards of respect for elders and ancestors, both grandmother and grandfather are very important figures. We grandparents may have more status than we realize and greater obligations than we have assumed.

February 23, 1988

ॐ

You Can Teach Manners

Early in my career as a weekly contributor to these pages, I wrote a piece on the subject of good manners, which has achieved an all-time popularity rating with my readers.

It dealt with the fundamentals of good manners, as taught by grandmothers of another generation to their children, who are now the parents of adolescents to whom the article was directed.

"I've mailed copies of your editorial to my children who are at college, for you have written what I have preached to them for years," wrote one grateful mother. "Your defense of good manners came not one minute too soon," commented another. "The current generation fails to recognize that manners are as important today as they were in their grandparents' time. Thank you—maybe they'll believe you more than they have me."

Parents blame their children, but if I were placing it, I would be inclined to hold the mothers and fathers responsible for not having made their standards stick. I speak as a parent, as well as a writer, and it's my conviction that for a variety of reasons, from single-parent families to children who have become unresponsive to parental guidance, parents can raise the kind of children they want if they are willing to work hard enough at the task.

Improved manners came into popular usage as societies enlarged and became accustomed to living with each other. Good manners evolved over generations as the lubricant that helped inter-neighbor relations. Learning to say "thank you," and meaning it, costs nothing but pays rich dividends.

Politeness demonstrates a concern for others, and is quickly recompensed by the recipients. Though the basic principles of good manners were developed in the past centuries, some of the elements have proved, over time, to be unnecessary, while others are just as valid as when they were first used. Every child should be accorded the opportunity to challenge the customs of the past, but should not be given the privilege of a blanket veto to reject them across the board.

The manners we learn in our youth grow up to be the best business practices of today. Business manners are the compendium of individual manners. Offspring who grow up refusing to write thank-you notes for gifts and who disdain ordinary rules of courtesy will become the kind of business leaders who follow similar habits in the conduct of their companies.

From personal experience as the chief executive officer of a large company, I found that the use of "thank you" made my business associates happier and more pleasant to me and to our customers. I discovered that the policy of prompt replies to complaint letters, queries and compliments was universally appreciated by the recipients.

A letter to the editor of these pages from a resident of Arlington, Texas, complained that he had answered 206 employment ads that ran in *The Dallas Morning News* and had received acknowledgments from only 2 percent of the advertisers to inform him that the position had been filled or stating that he lacked proper qualifications.

This is one egregious example of corporate bad manners, which I hope is the exception and not the rule, for it is a rejection of the best personal and business rule I have ever learned—the Golden Rule.

Business executives might do well to review corporate correspondence replies to job applicants and letters of complaint to determine whether the reputation of the company is being enhanced or tarnished.

August 25, 1992

♫

Maybe Politeness Is Making a Comeback

For a long time, I have had concern about the decline in social decorum or just plain decency, as evidenced by the failure of people to write notes of appreciation for gifts, meals or favors.

The actual notes or telephone calls are secondary to getting the information that the gifts were received. Gratitude isn't my objective. I just think it is part of polite conduct to express thanks promptly.

I know I run the risk of being labeled old-fashioned for such dogma, but if my concern is old-fashioned, then so be it.

Although some of my own grandchildren have been included in the ranks of the "non-communicators," I am glad to state I am making progress as the result of repeated discussion with them. But grandchildren are by no means the only offenders, for some business acquaintances are equally tardy in expressing appreciation.

101

Business schools that confer MBAs on their graduates would do well to add a brief course on social etiquette to acquaint them with the accepted standards of polite society.

This year's crop of prompt Christmas thank-yous was encouraging, with a response rate of about 80 percent, compared to 50 percent just four years ago. I was particularly heartened by two letters—one from a 15-year-old boy, the other from a young man of 22 years.

The first letter was from the son of a friend we see perhaps once a year but to whom we have been sending a modest Christmas remembrance since he was 5. This is the first time he has written, and we were pleased by both his courtesy and the clarity and sincerity of his thank-you letter. The other, briefer note was from one of the valet car parkers at a building I frequently visit.

Both letters were unlikely to have been initiated by parents. I was glad to learn the two young men's gifts had survived the annual mail crunch and changes of address.

Perhaps we are entering a new era in which some elements of 19th-century social usage will come back into favor. Many customs need to be reviewed and retired from usage because they are out of date and no longer applicable to current lifestyles.

But politeness, as exemplified in verbal and written form, is just as essential as it was when mankind first became civilized.
January 30, 1996

Silence Can Be Golden

Among the numerous privileges of living in this country is the right of free expression. However, the Bill of Rights fails to provide any guidelines on how long a citizen has the right to talk.

When individuals gather to listen to someone speak, there is an undeclared agreement to remain silent, unless they disagree so violently that they decide to boo.

The right to chat *sotto voce* is abrogated during a theatrical performance, a symphony program, a graduation exercise, a funeral or any occasion when the ability of others to listen is curtailed by distracting sounds.

Most of us have observed the unwillingness of an orchestra's conductor to begin a program when he hears distracting coughs, sneezes or laughter in the music hall. He will stand impassively with his back to the audience, his arms outstretched, waiting for quiet and tranquility to prevail. He knows the audience shouldn't be deprived of the right to listen without competition from extraneous sounds.

Audiences occasionally object to this demonstration of power, but it is the conductor's prerogative to demand a quiet house, just as it is a pilot's prerogative to require all passengers to be seated before he moves the plane from the ramp.

All of this commentary was sparked by a recent civic luncheon, at which there seemed to be some confusion over who had been invited to speak—the toastmaster and honoree or some members of the audience. The honoree was visibly confused by the chattering, while the other guests were irritated by their gabby neighbors.

The simple act of buying a banquet ticket entitles the guest to receive food and to listen but not to compete with those on the dais. Even the famed Supreme Court Justice Oliver Wendell Holmes once declared, "Screaming 'fire' in a crowded theater upon discovery of a blaze is not only freedom of speech but a dutiful exercise of citizenship. If there is no fire, the call is not freedom of expression but, rather, license."

As the writer of Ecclesiastes cautioned, "There is an appointed time for everything, and there is a time for every event under heaven—a time to be silent and a time to speak." On occasion, silence can be golden.

April 30, 1996

Separation Can Be Healthy for Marriage

Perfectly happy married couples enjoy an occasional separation from each other for a few days or even a week or two. Enid Nemmy, a writer for the *New York Times*, once made a study of what women do when their husbands are away.

She discovered that many women not only like, but look forward to, being left alone for a brief period. This may come as a shock to some husbands, but the solo time is generally considered as a mini-vacation. The biggest attraction of a few days apart, Miss Nemmy reported, is the opportunity to slop around, eat or not eat as mood dictates, go to bed at 7 p.m. or 7 a.m.—or, preferably, a combination of all three.

One woman interviewed said, "When he's away, it's my big chance to get in bed and eat. My husband has three rules: no eating, smoking or television in bed. It's also wonderful, because I don't have to fix dinner or go out to dinner. Sometimes I give myself a facial mask; it might scare my husband if he were around."

Another woman stated that her husband's trips gave her "a chance to catch up on myself, my own thinking, my own ideas and my own friends. Sometimes I visit with girlfriends he may not particularly enjoy, or I'll go to museums, lectures or movies he may not like. The biggest bonus is to read until 3 a.m. or turn on the television at any hour."

What these women are saying, it seems to me, is that marriage brings with it a loss of privacy to both parties, a quality most of us need, although in varying degrees. Short separations provide for an indulgence in both privacy and selfishness, which if taken for brief periods are like tonics, both salutary and non-habit forming.

After all, husbands have been doing identical things for ages: the hunting trips with the boys, the weekly poker games, Sunday golf and Monday night football are all devices that provide breaks from the routine of marriage.

When wives go off on trips, many husbands may find that it's difficult to find the can opener, or to identify which knob turns on the oven. Home is apt to have a very vacant quality without a wife to make it habitable, which is another way of saying that it's the wife who makes a house into a home.

Short absences can have a very absolute effect on marriages, providing a deeper sense of appreciation to both parties. The obvious conclusion from this little survey is that we need to reduce these impressions to statistics to determine their validity. That's going to require further research.

Routines may be comfortable habits, but may very well become like calluses that damage sensitivity, a necessary ingredient for successful marriage.

January 4, 1994

ॐ

Short Memory Aids Marriage

As a nonagenarian, I have discovered that some young people mistakenly consider me a fount of knowledge on a number of subjects, such as one posed to me just last week: "What are the factors that contribute to a happy marriage?" It is a question that has been argued for generations, possibly as long as the institution of marriage has existed.

Forbearance has been suggested as a vital ingredient. So have a willingness to compromise, an even temper and a happy disposition. All have been in the glossary of marriage counselors. Certainly, they are qualities that would be recognized as helping to make a marriage work more smoothly.

As a happily married man, I make no bones about the fact that marriage can be a very taxing institution. It takes a strong, determined couple to make it work. That, of course, is one reason for the high rate of divorce.

The fact that couples, desperately in love at the outset, become irreparably alienated shouldn't come as a surprise. It is quite remarkable that two people from completely different backgrounds, and brought up with contradictory value systems, ever can make the grade as happy, lifelong companions.

Only in societies with extraordinary familial pressures, reinforced by the mores of the community, can divorce be successfully resisted. In India, where marriages still are arranged by the parents and where there is no opportunity of dissent by either prospective partner, the divorce rate is 2 percent.

The quality that probably is most important in happy marriages, but seldom mentioned, is a short memory. At first, that doesn't seem logical, for one could argue that an accurate memory would lead to bliss, providing recollections of successes.

On the other hand, a long memory also recalls past grievances, petty disputes and differences of opinions that can become constant irritants if one allows them. Those endowed with a short memory are able to forget minor slights to the ego and irritating reminders of minor spats. Nothing in life can be perfect, and certainly a long memory that remembers everything and forgets nothing can destroy almost any marriage.

So, my advice is to allow yourself to be *put upon* occasionally. It will help perpetuate your marriage.

It was Winston Churchill who said, "Democracy is the worst form of government, except all those other forms that have been tried from time to time." If put to it, he also might have said, "Marriage is the worst of all human institutions, except for all the others that are worse."

June 6, 1995

106

Music Reflects the Times

A review that *Time* magazine published a dozen years ago, of the performance of a newly discovered Mozart symphony, always has stuck in my memory. It stated, "While a vogue is transient, music is not." As usual, *Time* is most wrong when it is most pontifical.

The notion that music is timeless is a recent one. None of the arts is more transitory than music. For one reason, music changes drastically with the available technology. Compare, for example, the hurdy-gurdy of the medieval minstrel with the electric guitar of Mick Jagger. Yet both epitomized the popular tastes of their era.

Even the timeless Mozart concert, which the *Time* reviewer hailed, shows this dependence on technology. The 9-year-old Mozart wrote the symphony for the delicate sound of the harpsichord. Even then, harpsichords were being supplanted by the pianoforte, literally the "soft-loud" instrument.

That was only partly true, because musicians were intrigued by the greater dynamic range of the piano. The harpsichord also was the victim of the spirit of democracy that swept Europe during Mozart's time. After the French Revolution, many harpsichords were chopped up for firewood because they were symbols of the hated aristocracy.

Fortunately, our generation of musicians has rediscovered the harpsichord. If the performer of the *Time*-reviewed performance had used a piano instead, the new Mozart symphony might have sounded harsh to the ears of its reviewer.

There is no reason to expect that music should be any more eternal than literature or visual art. All of the arts are expressions of the times in which they are produced. If successful, they either reflect the current artistic standards of their times or they forecast incipient changes, not always easily visible to the understanding of the majority.

It is the latter that gets creative artists in trouble. If they are too far ahead of their times, the mass public will reject them and their works. If timed closer to actuality, the creators become elevated to the roles of heroes.

To test the veracity of this concept, think back to the time that jazz, and then rock, first offended the ears of listeners. William Faulkner shocked the eyes of the readers of the mid-20th century; Jackson Pollock aroused public ire by his dribblings in the 1950s; and the compositions of Bartok and Mahler still disturb as many ears as they please.

Most people don't know that in the Middle Ages music was written for one performance only. To repeat a performance would have been as unthinkable to a Medici as serving leftovers at a banquet.

December 3, 1991

ATURE

Spring Brightens Our View

Even the most fervent fans of Georgia O'Keeffe's paintings wouldn't subscribe to the artist's reputed evaluation of flowers. Her attributed statement, "I hate flowers—I paint them because they're cheaper than models and they don't move," sounds like her brusque and often brutally frank reply to questions from reporters. Of course, Miss O'Keeffe was incorrect, for flowers do move as they unfold in a vase, even after having endured acute surgery.

At no time of the year do flowering plants and trees reward us more than in the spring when the landscape bursts into full color. Carefully planned gardens vie with the rogue volunteers that adorn the fields and roadsides. Sedate and somber trees explode with a violent display of blossoms to proclaim they have survived the vigor of winter and have returned once again from a period of dormancy.

This annual celebration of the changing of the seasons, aided and abetted often by the helping hands of cultivation, is one of the most triumphant periods of the whole year. It is a fitting reward for humans who have been able to survive the vicissitudes of rains and mudslides, snow and ice, tornadoes and drought.

Nature gives this salute to all mankind and, in turn, receives the profuse appreciation from young and old, rich and poor, sophisticated gardeners and dubbers alike. It is commonplace to comment that there is no such thing as a free lunch in life, but nature's munificence probably comes closer than any other occurrences to provide us with a luscious repast without a cent of contribution.

As a result of this intense color and fragrance extravaganza, we are stimulated to plant not only on our own property, but also in public areas, on highway median strips, in front of private buildings with garden spaces and in window boxes.

We choose to remember the ill and frail, as well as the healthy, with floral gifts and trees. As a matter of fact, there is no more glorious memorial to those departed than the gift of a tree or a grove of trees to organizations that will care for them, such as the Dallas Arboretum and Botanical Gardens on Garland Road, where the gardens at this very moment are in full bloom and on display for one and all to enjoy. *Dallas Blooms* is one of the best shows in Dallas, not only in the spring but throughout the year.

Georgia O'Keeffe would have enjoyed it.

April 4, 1995

Sense of Scale Helps Neighborhoods

Years ago, there was a great deal of discussion about limitations on the size of homes that could be placed on city lots. There were restrictions on the percentage of a lot that a home could occupy, as well as restrictions on how near a home could be built to the sidewalk or the curb.

Those regulations varied from street to street, depending on the requirements laid down in the original property deeds. Some of the restrictions applied to designated neighborhoods and particular developments.

The wisdom of those stipulations shows up today as we see builders invading neighborhoods of small houses and erecting structures larger than the norm. All of which leads one to wonder whatever happened to those requirements.

The radical difference in scale between the original homes and the newcomers is aesthetically upsetting. The result is streets of small houses interspersed with monsters two or three times their size. The mega-houses give the appearance of having muscled their way in through brute force.

Scale is an element of design not well understood by many designers and by even fewer homeowners. Among the cities that have consistently controlled scale are Paris and Amsterdam and, in this country, Boston and Austin.

The resizing of homes on small lots may very well be within the legal regulations, but the mixture of grandiose houses and modest ones is imposing a new look on whole neighborhoods. Big and little homes don't mix well.

The owner of a small house receives a flattering offer and agrees to sell. One mega-house moves in. Then another owner of a small house succumbs to a tempting price. Very quickly, the whole street gets an unbalanced look. The smaller houses appear to shrink next to their neighbors who have built houses too large for their lots.

There are, of course, valid economic reasons that this process has developed and accelerated. They have to do with the demand for land in the Park Cities and North Dallas. Families with young children are eager to send them to the Highland Park and University Park schools and to the adjacent Dallas schools.

Also, building height restrictions have prohibited multistoried apartment buildings and low-rise apartment zoning in those areas, so economic demand has put the pressure on single-family residential lots.

The net effect is that a large number of long-time residents on some nice streets in the Park Cities and Dallas have had their vision of residential life shattered, and the cities themselves have lost some of their charm.

Too bad!

July 22, 1997

Nonconformists Play a Vital Role

Anatole Broyard, the distinguished critic who writes for the *New York Times Book Review*, suggests that the popularity of biographies of authors indicates a hunger in our lives for intense personalities. This raises a worthy subject for speculation.

"Why are biographies of writers so popular now?" Mr. Broyard asks. "It's our need to read about intense personalities," he speculates. And since writers aren't currently painting their heroes larger than life, we satisfy this need by reading about the writer instead of what he has written. This leads to the peculiar phenomenon of books about Lord Byron being more popular than books by Lord Byron.

There's no question that Lord Byron was an intense personality. Pressured by the notoriety of many spectacular love affairs, he ran off to Italy, where he fathered an illegitimate daughter, joined a free-love commune and dabbled in revolutionary politics. Relating this to the present day is the fact that many of our acquaintances have had a son, a nephew or a friend of a friend who did much the same thing.

Why read a biography of Lord Byron when you can just pick up the phone for the latest gossip? Lord Byron's life might have shocked the Victorians, but to us, he was just a little ahead of his time. So, among the people I know anyway, hunger for intensity can't be the reason for the trend toward biographies of writers. Maybe we're not looking for intensity so much as reassurance.

If Lord Byron, Katherine Anne Porter, Norman Mailer or Paul Theroux could pull all these crazy stunts and still produce worthwhile works of a lasting value, maybe there's hope for our black sheep who are still grazing unfettered and unabashed in the pastures of nonconformity.

Whoever developed the notion that nonconformity was bad, anyway? True, society always has preferred conformity because it was neater, more tidy, less troublesome. Actually, we need a modicum of nonconformists to stimulate new solutions for all sorts of subjects, from science to morals. Nonconformists may make us think enough to sustain our own values.

We used to call them "characters." When I was a boy, we sort of snickered at them, but secretly we held them in a certain kind of awe because they dared to be different.

My own guess about why writers' biographies are popular is that we hope to gain from those nonconformists some guidance for coping with the problems in our own lives. We like them because they dared to be different.

July 19, 1988

ॐ

Mavericks Add Spice to Our Lives

According to the dictionary, a maverick is "an independent individual who refuses to conform with his group."

An article in the *Wall Street Journal* stated that the word "maverick" originated with Samuel Maverick, a 19th-century Texas rancher who refused to brand his cattle. Unbranded cattle thus came to be called "mavericks." It wasn't until later, when Mr. Maverick's independent-minded grandson, Maury, went to Congress, that the term came to describe people, too.

Today, the word "maverick" is still used to describe people who go their own way, people who stray from the beaten path.

As the *Journal* put it, "Mavericks include free spirits, loners, idealistic reformers and rogues. They tend to be their own worst enemies. They often walk fine lines of principle, which only they

114

discern. They often champion foredoomed causes, yet stubbornly they refuse to change. Probably they couldn't change if they wanted to."

I, for one, wouldn't want them to change.

Mavericks are the world's inventors, innovators and artists. They're the naive Mr. Smiths in Frank Capra's famous movie *Mr. Smith Goes to Washington.*

And mavericks are the perfect counterbalance for people who are too serious, too set in their ways. They bring life to everyday situations, fresh perspectives to humdrum practices. They add humor, color and idealism, qualities that most of us find to be in short supply.

There are feminine mavericks in matters of dress. They refuse the edicts of the fashion dictators and wear their skirts at lengths they enjoy and consider most becoming.

There are male mavericks who dare to wear beards in a clean-shaven environment, either because they prefer the look or think they gain distinction from the masses. Or simply because they dislike the chore of a daily shave.

There are mavericks in every field—writing, music, business. Some of them fall by the wayside, but others find that their strange ideas eventually meet with public acceptance, and they become accepted as VIPs. We used to call them "characters," those who chose to be, or found themselves, different from their daily associates.

Our current culture tends to encourage standardization of people and merchandise, with the result that there is less recognition of the value of those who dissent, who march to a different drummer. Mass production and distribution have been responsible to a great extent for the uniformity of consumer products.

Mavericks are vital in every walk of life, be it politics, business or education. They're the people who ask questions, who take nothing for granted.

And that makes us all think.

January 7, 1992

Some Odds Can't Be Beaten

Those who take a cautious approach to life are forever advising us to buckle our seat belts, lose thirty pounds and avoid dark alleys. "It doesn't always happen to the other guy," they warn. That's not quite true.

Deep in our hearts, we know it's not always the other fellow who reaps what he brought on himself if he ignores health and safety precautions. So we reluctantly give up delicious, irresponsible and unhealthy habits, knowing that even if the odds are with us, some awful things *can* happen to us.

But there's something wrong here. How many of us win the lottery, the long shot at the race track or even the raffle of a Rolls-Royce? Yet a surprising number of us get struck by lightning. The way life works out, if the odds are 50-to-1 that you'll win the Saturday night Bingo game, you'll get mugged every time. Obviously, there's something else working besides blind chance.

You don't agree? All right, let's take an easy one, and I'll try to convince you. Let's choose an example where the odds are theoretically 50-50. You're at the bank, the airline ticket counter or the supermarket and there are two lines. If the world were fair, wouldn't you pick the faster-moving line at least half the time? But it never happens.

You know as well as I do that the short wait always happens to the other guy. You can even go about it scientifically, observing before you choose your line. You note the average speed of transaction, the mood of the clerk, the probable workload offered by your fellow customers. You can even try to cheat fate by making your logical deduction and then choosing the *other* line. Still, the line you ultimately commit yourself to is always the slowest. I wish the statisticians would quit kidding us and admit it.

If you are skeptical, make a list of the lines in which you find yourself most often—the post office, D/FW Airport exit line, the box offices at any of the sporting events. Even try standing in the line with a rabbit's foot or a four-leaf clover in your pocket.

I was never much of a gambler, getting all the thrills I needed from the chancy business of retailing. But if anybody of that inclination came up with a system to beat the longest-line odds, I'd be interested.

December 10, 1985

੨ﬞ

Pencils Tell a Lot About Us

When was the last time you used a pencil? Unless you're an accountant, a crossword puzzle addict or a kid below the age of twelve, you probably can't remember. The poet would have us believe that the pen is mightier than the sword, but, in my opinion, you can learn far more about an individual's personality from the pencil. The ordinary wooden pencil that most of us use can be an accurate psychological clue.

The first written mention of the pencil dates from 1565. The discovery of a large vein of graphite had just made a pencil in every pocket a possibility. Today, though, that 400-year-old writing instrument isn't all that popular. Perhaps it's because the pencil's markings aren't permanent enough or because using a pencil is an admission that you might make a mistake.

Frankly, I like pencils. They're plain and practical, not gimmicky. Have you ever heard of a designer pencil or seen a pencil with an alligator on it? I especially like those bright, yellow-orange No. 2 pencils, the kind you used to take tests with when you were in grade school. And, like all good pencils, they never smeared or skipped or ruined a perfectly good sheet of Big Chief tablet paper.

In revealing personalities, for example, a pencil with a worn-down eraser shows that the user spends a great deal of time erasing. Perhaps this means he's dissatisfied with what he's written. Maybe he had difficulty making a decision or felt a little unsure of himself. If you see a pencil with a long shaft and a short eraser in combination, the owner may be a perfectionist, a very picky person who writes little but erases a lot. A stubby shaft and a long eraser may indicate signs of a genius, or at least someone who believes he never makes a mistake.

Teeth marks on a pencil? A sure sign of worry. Sharpened at both ends? An efficiency expert, or a penny pincher. A red pencil? An editor. Colored pencils? An artist or illustrator.

Another thing I like about pencils is that they're great for breaking when you're frustrated. Bic pens just don't have the same snap. Pencils are well behaved too. If there's lead in them, they write. Put one behind your ear, and it stays there until you need it. There's only one thing that bothers me about pencils, and that is their erasers. They always run out before the pencil does. Nothing is more useless than a nice, tall, well-sharpened pencil without an eraser.

Since pencil sharpeners are now standard equipment, everyone starts out even with a sharp pencil, and that is what we are often told makes the deal.

June 5, 1990

∂

A World Without Shmoo

If a poll were taken today, I doubt that more than 5 percent of those interviewed could identify a "Shmoo."

Some people have reached the age at which they have erased extraneous information from their brain cells, while others are so young that they never have heard of the word.

A Shmoo is an animal that never existed—except in the imagination of one of our most creative comic artists, the late Al Capp. It appeared in *Li'l Abner*, together with a cast of characters whose names were as recognized as those of the most famous movie personalities of that era.

There were, of course, Li'l Abner (the lead juvenile), Daisy Mae (his adoring girlfriend), Lonesome Polecat (the Indian), Hairless Joe, Joe Bftspik (the little unhappy guy with a dark cloud over his head), General Bullmoose (the ultimate capitalist), Fearless Fosdick and the Shmoo.

A Shmoo was everyone's dream animal. It was plump and cuddly, companionable and cooperative. It multiplied its species instantaneously; it couldn't be exterminated. It delivered ham and eggs or laid bottle grade-A milk.

Shmoos sacrificed themselves willingly. As one writer put it, "When broiled, they tasted like sirloin steak, and when fried, like chicken. They reproduced so prodigiously, they threatened to wreck the economy."

They were too good to be true. Mr. Capp summarized their virtues in a strip on Shmoos in which a character observes, "It's the worst tragedy that ever hit hoomanity—be'in overwhelmed by pure unadulterated goodness!!"

In his definitive book, *Great Comic Strip Artists*, Richard Marshall wrote, "The lovable Shmoo was a creature that fulfilled everyone's whims, from the desire for romantic companionship to the desire for a plate of ham and eggs."

He went on the explain: "These charming creatures were not boons to Li'l Abner's world—they were menaces. Society could not tolerate the amity and harmony they brought. The Shmoos were beaten back into the Valley of the Shmoon by the people that preferred a world ruled not by the truth but by prevarication.

"Many great cartoonists had made their reputations by cleverly ridiculing society and illuminating the foibles of human nature . . . but none was as sardonic as Capp. Couched in outlandish fun, his statements were harsh.

120

"Capp was calling society absurd, not silly; human nature not simply misguided but irredeemably and irreducibly corrupt. Unlike any other strip and indeed unlike many other pieces of literature, the comic strip *Li'l Abner* was more than a satire of the human condition. It was a commentary upon human nature itself."

John Steinbeck called Al Capp the best satirist since 18th-century British writer Laurence Sterne. Others compared him to François Rabelais. In any event, his most memorable satire remains that of the universal foibles of the human condition—pomposity, lust, greed, power and intolerance.

September 9, 1997

HOBIAS

Those Obscure Phobias

Do you ever feel jealous of fashionable friends who brag
about being in psychoanalysis? Well, cheer up. Could be there's
something wrong with you, like an obscure phobia. A phobia is
an abnormal, sometimes incapacitating, fear. This is not to be
confused with normal, everyday worries. No, phobias are deep-
rooted anxieties that can render their victims frozen with fear.

Phobias, of course, are more than just aversions; they are deep-
felt, psychic-resistance forces that cause great trauma and pain to
those who suffer from them. According to *An Abomination of
Phobias*, there are thousands of different anxieties. Read this list
and see if you recognize any personal problem area.

Have you ever come down with a serious case of hamartophobia?
I suspect that not many of us could honestly claim we have.
Hamartophobia is the fear of sin. If you're afraid of sex, you're the
unfortunate victim of genophobia. There is a name for the fear of
seeing animal teeth. That's odontophobia.

Some phobias actually sound like the fears they're describing,
like the fear of staircases, climacophobia, and the fear of making
decisions, decidophobia.

We all sometimes show symptoms of ergasophobia, the fear of
work, and algophobia, the fear of pain.

Some of the more commonplace phobias are xenophobia, the
fear of strangers; claustrophobia, the fear of being enclosed;
necrophobia, the fear of dead bodies; and acrophobia, the fear of
heights.

Less familiar ones that we don't encounter frequently are
belonephobia, the fear of pins and needles; eremophobia, the

123

fear of being alone; and taphephobia, the fear of being buried alive.

There are those who fear opening their eyes, which is termed otophobia. Some people have astrophobia, the fear of lightning and thunder; trichophobia, the fear of hair; Francophobia, the fear of France or anything French; and lyssophobia, a morbid fear of hydrophobia.

Worst of all I guess is to be afflicted with phobophobia, the fear of one's own fears! The best advice comes from *The People's Almanac*: "The best thing you can do today is to hope you won't develop iatrophobia, the fear of doctors, so you can still be cured, that is, if your friendly, neighborly physician doesn't develop the fear of phobic patients."

May 24, 1988

Needed: A Visionary Planner

In 1910, Dallas had no focus. It had numerous railways that traversed through the middle of the town, each with its independent station.

The Houston and Texas Central, the first railroad to come to Dallas, traversed what is now Central Expressway. Its terminal was on Pacific Avenue just east of the present expressway. The Santa Fe ran north along the Scottish Rite Cemetery to its station, which was on the site of the current Federal Building on Commerce Street.

The Katy came through northeast Dallas to its terminal, located on the fringe of what is now Pacific and Record streets. The Texas and Pacific went along Pacific, dividing the downtown into two parts. It shared one station with the Houston and Texas Central and had a second downtown terminal at Lamar Street.

To get to Oak Cliff, buggies and cars climbed up the two-year-old viaduct to get over the train tracks and the normally quiescent, mosquito-infested Trinity River. The Trinity was a problem. When it flooded, the water could reach the courthouse. Once it got so high that the City Hall (now the site of the Adolphus Hotel) was threatened.

Getting around town was difficult because of the railroad tracks and the absence of through streets running north and south. The town had no shape, form or focus.

George Bannerman Dealey, publisher of *The Dallas Morning News*, and a group of citizens recognized the situation and invited the eminent city planner George Kessler to come to Dallas and take a look at its problems. Kessler previously had laid out a plan for the State Fairgrounds, so he had some familiarity with the town.

He dealt with the fundamental problems, starting with the Trinity River and the downtown area. He recommended that levees be installed, and he suggested that several downtown streets be extended and that some new ones be constructed.

Kessler also urged eliminating the dangerous Texas and Pacific tracks on Pacific and making the right of way into a boulevard to Fair Park (a fragment of which was done after a thirteen-year fight was settled by a Supreme Court decision).

White Rock Lake was a result of his recommendation for the location of a needed water reservoir and a surrounding park.

These were some of the accomplishments of the gifted Kessler. Others were stymied by reluctant landowners. Dealey died, and Dallas lost its vision of becoming a city. It eventually happened, but not as a result of having followed a well-thought-out design.

Kessler was a visionary. He had a great appreciation for the value of parkways and would have fought to preserve some that were sold. Dallas lost an enormous asset through carelessness. But Kessler's plan was naive in some respects, too. It lacked consistency and character at its northern limits and seemed improvised at a number of junctions.

Still, the Kessler plan proposed sweeping and dramatic aspirations for the town. He held up a vision of how Dallas should grow. He gave weight to the city's overall appearance and to strong visual links between areas, as well as to functional solutions to problems.

Kessler was the right man for Dallas at that time. Dallas needs a planner of stature now, a combination of visionary and pragmatist who can help solve some of the problems that have resulted from a failure to follow good planning principles.

The past is past; the future is ahead. What Dallas needs is a return to comprehensive planning as it attempts to deal with the problems created by the automobile and the wants and needs of its residents.

. This is a subject worthy of immediate and serious consideration

126

by the City Council, the Dallas Chamber of Commerce, the Citizens Council and other groups interested in the future of the city.
August 4, 1987

$\mathscr{P}$REDICTIONS

Some Gloriously Wrongheaded Predictions

Book reviewers are subject to the same statistical success in picking winners as sports writers and editors of high school annuals.

That is the undeclared thesis of a charming little book by Bill Henderson titled *Rotten Reviews*, which was published last year by the Pushcart Press. It should be required reading for all book reviewers who may be overly impressed by their own judgmental powers, or by an inherent desire to squelch.

On second thought, it should be recommended to critics in all fields—music, architecture, politics and fashion.

Take, for example, a quote from a critical piece on Charles Dickens in the *Saturday Review*, 1858, in which the writer declared, "We do not believe in the permanencies of his reputation. Fifty years hence, most of his allusions will be harder to understand than those in *The Dunciad*, and our children will wonder what their ancestors meant by putting Mr. Dickens at the head of the novelists of his day." Last I heard, Dickens was still doing well in the bookstores and the theater.

In the *Atlantic Monthly* in 1892, American author Thomas Bailey Aldrich said of American poet Emily Dickinson: "An eccentric, dreary, half-educated recluse in an out-of-the-way New England village—or anywhere else—cannot with impunity set at defiance the laws of gravitation and grammar . . . oblivion lingers in the immediate neighborhood." It would seem that the writer was forgotten sooner than his subject.

Even T. S. Eliot had a hard time following the performance of *The Cocktail Party* at the Edinburgh Festival in 1949 when Alan

128

Dent, critic of the *News Chronicle*, gave the play the *coup de grace* by saying, "The week after—as well as the morning after—I take it to be nothing but a finely acted piece of flapdoodle."

Thomas Carlyle, in 1871, characterized Ralph Waldo Emerson as "a hairy-headed and toothless baboon." American critics have handled Emerson roughly, too, but never to the point of verbally caricaturing his appearance.

The French newspaper *Le Figaro* declared in 1857, apropos the new novel *Madame Bovary* by Gustave Flaubert, that "Monsieur Flaubert is not a writer."

F. Scott Fitzgerald had tough going in his homeland when he wrote *The Great Gatsby* in 1925. The *New York Herald* dismissed it by commenting, "What has never been alive cannot very well go on living. So this is a book of the season, only." A whole generation of readers thought differently.

The *Saturday Review of Literature* was obviously upset, for its review read, "Mr. F. Scott Fitzgerald deserves a good shaking . . . *The Great Gatsby* is an absurd story, whether considered as romance, melodrama, or plain record of New York high life."

Joseph Heller's *Catch 22* was misjudged by many of the reviewers when it was published in 1961, including a critic for the *New York Times* who found "It gasps for want of craft and sensibility . . . the book is an emotional hodgepodge; no mood is sustained long enough to register for more than a chapter." Readers obviously paid no attention to the reviewer's opinion, it is only fair to note.

All of the above reaffirms the old Chinese proverb that I repeat on any possible occasion: "Forecasting is a difficult business, particularly when it deals with matters of the future."

December 1, 1987

Predictions Gone Sour

Going down in history doesn't require heroic acts or noble deeds. Sometimes all it takes is having the strength of conviction and some pure, unmitigated gall. Often, oral predictions are not remembered after the fact, but written ones come back to haunt their authors.

No classification of scholars or public figure is immune from error or challenges to historic judgments. Artists, scientists, politicians and the clergy have contributed to nonsensical appraisals and foolish prophecies.

"Next to being right in this world, the best of all things is to be clearly and definitively wrong," wrote T. H. Huxley. That pronouncement is the cheery theme of *Facts and Fallacies—A Book of Definitive Mistakes and Misguided Predictions*, published by St. Martin's Press, and now, unfortunately, out of print. This celebration of glorious fatuity begins right at the beginning, "The earth was created in 4004 B.C. on Sunday, October 21, at 9:00 in the morning."

Well, who's really to say? The judgment errors of science can be just as mortifying as those of religion. In the late 19th century, Lord Kelvin, president of the Royal Society, predicted that heavier-than-air flying machines were impossible. He also predicted that radio had no future and that X-rays were a hoax. Kelvin wasn't the only one, though, whose judgments had more self-assurance than accuracy.

In 1956, Sir Richard Woolley, the astronomer royal of Britain, declared that space travel was "utter bilge." To err is ancient. He was joined in this opinion by Simon Newcastle, a celebrated astronomer, who declared, "Aerial flight is one of that class of problem with which men will never be able to cope."

George Bernard Shaw wrote to his author friend G. K. Chesterton in 1910 and stated, "When astronomers tell me that a star is so far off that its light takes a thousand years to reach, the magnitude of the lie seems to me inartistic."

That great sage, Adolf Hitler, referred to his Nazi Party revolution, saying, "By this revolution, the German way of life is definitely settled for the next 1,000 years."

The futurist John Langdon-Davis of England held that "by 1975 parents will have ceased to bring up their children in private family units," and "by 1966 work will be limited to three hours a day," and optimistically predicted, "Crime will be considered a disease after 1981 and will cease to exist by A.D. 2000."

Even as great an inventor as Thomas Edison sold electricity short when he concluded, "There is no plea which will justify the use of high tension and alternating controls either in a scientific or commercial sense. They are employed solely to reduce investments in copper wire and real estate."

And the great chewing gum magnate and owner of the Chicago Cubs labeled nighttime ball games "just a fad, passing fancy." None other than the renowned writer T. S. Eliot observed, "Football has become so complicated that the student will find it a recreation to go to class."

Samuel Johnson postulated to James Boswell, "Sir, nature has given woman so much power that the law cannot afford to give her more," and even the ancients of biblical times missed their forecasts, for in Ecclesiastes it is claimed, "There is no new thing under the sun."

December 22, 1991

❧

Prophecy an Uncertain Art

Packing up to move across town to my new residence, I ran across an old *Life* magazine from 1954 predicting the major trends for our country for the next quarter-century. You'll be surprised, as I was, at the hits—and the misses.

Life's forecaster was George R. Harrison, then dean of the School of Sciences at Massachusetts Institute of Technology. I was surprised to discover that his predictions were right about as often as they were wrong. In building, for example, he predicted correctly that homes and office buildings would use more glass, and that construction workers would make more than $4 an hour. He thought, however, that downtown buildings would be shorter, never dreaming of New York's World Trade Center with its twin towers of 110 floors, Dallas' NationsBank Plaza with 72 floors, or Los Angeles' high-rise-studded skyline.

Mr. Harrison correctly called the increasing growth of the suburbs, but thought we'd be smart enough to build public transportation to whisk people from perimeter parking lots to their downtown jobs, and he didn't foresee the migration from suburbs *back* to the city. That might not have happened, though, if we'd solved our traffic problems. He knew we'd have little resistance to hopping a frequently scheduled, coast-to-coast or international jetliner, although he thought we'd arrive a little faster than we do. He was wrong when he thought we'd have nuclear-powered passenger airplanes by now. He foresaw our growing need to produce protein more efficiently, but thought we'd learn to love algae, not tofu.

He predicted the phenomenal growth of the chemical companies, as synthetics permeated our lives, but overlooked the coming importance of computers, then in their bulky, vacuum-tube infancy. He did not foresee the growing antipathy to hazardous chemical crop sprays. He refused to even speculate about space travel, calling it a "scientific plaything." He warned that his predicted trends would hold only if energy continued to be plentiful, but he didn't anticipate the Organization of Petroleum Exporting Countries.

The most unsettling thing about Mr. Harrison's predictions is the realization of how little time has passed since things that we take for granted now—like jet travel and plastic food wrap—were mere speculation.

May 24, 1994

 RINTING

Printing Is Nowhere Near Death

From the time of Gorgeous George, *I Married Joan* and Edward R. Murrow, people have been predicting the demise of printing. Now, though, printing is stronger than ever for some less-than-obvious reasons.

Ever since Johann Gutenberg invented movable typesetting in the 16th century, the printed word has been the most popular and efficient method of communicating information and ideas. Even if television and computers are replacing books, even in some classrooms, they haven't replaced printing.

The printed word is having a resurgence of popularity, as special-interest magazines and community newspapers proliferate, but the real area of explosion in printing is not in words but in graphics. Recent innovations in full-color printing techniques have made creative design at a reasonable cost in everything from embossed business cards to billboards. Even carpet patterns are being printed to help reduce the cost of broadloom.

People who haven't bought a book since they struggled through *Moby Dick* in high school form a ready market for colorful printed posters. The variety is endless, since many printers are discovering that a modest investment can convert a photograph or a painting into a high-quality product on good paper.

Also appealing to collectors is another kind of graphic printing—the small, private presses that are turning out exquisitely printed books, frequently on handmade paper. Even though they may not contain as many words as *War and Peace*, they can be considered as graphic art, because they are designed to be seen and admired, as well as to be read. They're snapped up at high

133

prices by knowledgeable collectors who realize their value will appreciate.

Commercially, printing is used for circuit boards as a time-saving device in the construction of intricate and minuscule electric panels. Nowhere, though, has printing contributed more to the handling of inventories, as has been the use of bar-coding on items of all categories. To keep accurate track of corpses in morgues, bar-coding on the foot of a dead person avoids mix-ups.

As an avid book collector, I am most appreciative of fine printing, but I am also an author, so I can't help feeling a little sad that—all else being equal—the more valuable book is the one described in the catalogues as being *mint*—one that has never been read! April 26, 1994

Don't Make Things Hard to Read

We tend to think of communications as being oral, but actually more of them come in printed form. There are instruction manuals, newspapers, magazines, advertisements, highway signs, restaurant menus, signs in stores and museums, and warning notices that flash on in automobiles. In many instances, the communication fails to get the message across quickly and easily.

Scientific studies at Cambridge University have established the principle that the eye will do a limited amount of reading of poorly designed texts. The eye balks at overly lengthy lines of type or eccentric typographical patterns. We remember less of a badly designed message than a reader-friendly one.

Acute examples of bad writing are found in manuals for computers, cameras and other technical appliances. They are so obtuse that they seem to have been written to discourage first-time users. They appear to have been written in technical jargon for the cognoscenti. Many potential buyers of computers and related devices suspect that the manuals' message is: "This isn't for you; the use of this machine is far above your intellectual capability."

The majority of museums in this country and abroad have failed to recognize that information about art objects needs to be located at a place convenient for the viewer's eyes. The best of such installations are at the Metropolitan Museum in New York and in some of the new galleries at the Dallas Museum of Art.

Restaurants frequently are guilty of printing menus that are difficult to read in daylight and impossible to decipher in subdued candlelight. Here again, the best menus are those that are simple typographically and printed on white paper with black ink.

No store does a better job of informational signing than Crate and Barrel. Its signs provide answers to customers' questions on virtually all of the merchandise on display. That saves time for both the sales staff and the customers.

Many automobiles have dashboard warning signs to call attention to fuel supplies and the need for checkups on certain systems. That is a nice service, but occasionally the driver is left in a state of panic when a flashing maintenance signal advises him to get the car to the shop when he is fifty miles from nowhere at midnight. "Soon as convenient!" would be a pleasant modification to the warning.

Highway signs have improved radically in recent years. Their green background and large, simple type make them easy to read. And successful billboards follow the basic principle that the best signs are like telegrams—brief messages in type large enough to be legible at fifty miles per hour.

In all of these examples, the common requirement for good communications is a message that the eye can read without undue effort.

January 21, 1997

135

ROVERBS

Proverbs Show a Society's Wisdom

As I pulled a book from a shelf in my library, a small red paper pamphlet fell out onto the floor. When I retrieved it, I found it was titled, "A Pocketful of Turkish Proverbs," excerpted from the *Archives of Texas Turkish Oral Narrative at Texas Tech University*. It had the inscription: "Passed on to Stanley Marcus on his 85th birthday by A. C. Greene."

Readers have responded well to the various lists I have published in my column. Perhaps this one will give them a further understanding of Turkish wisdom and humor. My appreciation, of course, goes to Mr. Greene, the perennial bibliophile, whom I thanked when I received it eight years ago.

Students of folklore and linguistics will find numerous duplications of religious and cultural ideas. The words may be different, but their meanings are the same.

Almost every culture makes some reference to "the good old days" when elders were the "wise men." Each culture pays homage to its older leaders. In Arizona, the Indian elders were labeled "Anasazi," or the "old ones." The tribe's elders were regarded as having learned the significance and meaning of time-hallowed habits, aphorisms, customs and observations about life that they could interpret for the youths of their communities.

If you are a book person, try to find books that are summaries of the wisdom of other cultures. Then identify common themes or needs with similar writings from the philosophies of old societies like China, Egypt, Thailand and even the United States.

A carefree head is to be found only on a scarecrow.

A full purse is one's best companion.

A knife wound heals, but a tongue wound festers.

A pound is 16 ounces wherever you go.

A visitor comes with ten blessings, eats one and leaves nine.

Activity breeds prosperity.

Better a calf of one's own than a jointly owned cow.

Do not roll up your trousers before reaching the stream.

Eat and drink with your friends but do not trade with them.

Fear an ignorant man more than a lion.

He gives twice who gives quickly.

If skill could be gained by watching, every dog would become
a butcher.

If you give him cloth, he will ask for the lining.

Of everything else, the newest; of friends, the oldest.

One never can repay one's debt to one's mother.

Part with your head but not with your secret.

Roses grow where a teacher hits.

The granary is at the point of the plowshare.

To speak is to sow; to listen is to reap.

What is loaned goes away smiling but returns weeping.

What the vineyard needs is hard work, not prayers.

Who buys cheap buys dear.

Whoever digs a pit for his neighbor should dig it his own size.

Work as if you were to live forever; live as if you were to die
tomorrow.

A wise man remembers his friends at all times; a fool, only
when he has need of them.

Do what your teacher says but not what he does.

For every wise man, there is one still wiser.

If you wish to do a good deed, consult no one.

One does not burn a blanket to get rid of a flea.

See with your mind; hear with your heart.

Stairs are climbed step by step.

Open your eyes, not your mouth.

May 26, 1998

 UALITY

List Changes in Quest for the Best

When I wrote *Quest for the Best*, I ended it with two lists—one of the "Best" and another of "Less than the Best." These selections, I must admit, were highly opinionated, but they represented my best current judgment.

In 1979, I listed as "Best" such things as London taxis, Sara Lee pound cake, the *New Yorker* magazine, Texas pink grapefruit, self-starters in cars, mangoes, the *MacNeil/Lehrer Report* and Levi jeans. I later added the Bic cigarette lighter, Famolare shoes, saltine crackers, Kleenex tissues, the *New York Times*, Scotch brand tape, the children's gift shop at the Metropolitan Museum of Art in New York, the Four Seasons Hotel in Washington, D.C., linguine alla vongole in Beverly Hills' La Scala Restaurant, Ma Bell, Teuscher chocolates from Switzerland, the entertainment of Joel Gray, the violin playing of Isaac Stern, nylon panty hose, Hermes ties and the comic strip *Peanuts*.

On the "Less than the Best" list, I had put such things as imitation furs, teased hair, single-width shoes, frilled tuxedo shirts, instant coffee, three-inch clogs, auto repair service, non-vine-ripened tomatoes and political promises. With greater experience, I then added New York taxicabs, the Los Angeles and John Wayne airports, synthetic whipped cream, Calvin Klein's sex-provocative blue jeans advertising, the Broadway musical *42nd Street*, Eastern's New York-to-Washington shuttle service, polyester bath towels and mats, airport souvenirs, Hawaiian floral shirts, fortune cookies and rose wines.

These lists are highly opinionated, but they are based on personal experiences. In a free-enterprise society, one of the privileges we enjoy is the right to make up our own minds about the quality of various products and services offered us. Advertising may sway us, but it can't convince us if we are not satisfied.

In retrospect, I think I either overvalued some of the things I listed as "Best" or else many of them didn't maintain their standards of quality. I would now move my evaluations of the Washington Four Seasons Hotel and Famolare shoes into the other category. On the other hand, most of those that I labeled "Less than the Best" haven't changed for the better.

Make up your own lists of what you find best and less than the best. This will help you to set your own standards, and you will find it an amusing way to spend your time as you wait in the doctor's office.

November 7, 1989

Bites We Shouldov Bitten

Charlie Schulz, cartoonist creator of *Peanuts*, long has been my nominee for the title of "Wisest Man in America." His sagacity is consistent. He is a reservoir of that scarce quality, common sense.

In a recent comic strip, Charlie Brown was asked, "Do you have any regrets?"

"Lots of them," he replied. Snoopy, who was lolling against a tree, added, "I regret the bites I should have bitten."

Those of us who have survived our youth could not in all honesty answer any differently than Charlie Brown and Snoopy. In retrospect, we are bound to have second thoughts on our deeds of commission and omission.

We may or may not go as far as Snoopy, but I suspect Snoopy may have been more honest in his admission. It is a truism to say life is full of uncertainties. Decisions that are based on a set of circumstances could well be different in another set of conditions.

"If I had only known that such and such would happen, I would have acted differently" is a feeble recognition that our foresight lacks the acuity of hindsight.

"I shouldov" and "I couldov" are bywords for every art collector to explain a failure to have purchased Henry Moore sculptures, or Renoir paintings, or a thousand other artists' works, when their prices were dirt cheap. The normal explanations for such misjudgments are incorrect evaluations of the artists' worth or lack of adequate resources to finance an acquisition. Business executives invoke the same phrases as they review lost opportunities to acquire rival enterprises or invade other markets before more visionary competitors took such steps.

Life is full of "shouldovs," but fortunately, most of us do make a sufficient number of correct decisions to help balance the failures of our vision.

Like Snoopy, all of us on occasion have taken our bites, but we generally ignore the times we did not stand up against bigotry, or attempts to control free expression by censorship, or oppression of minorities. We may have lacked courage, or perhaps we may have chosen not to be personally inconvenienced by being courageous. Those are some of "the bites we should have bitten."

As long as we still are alive, there is time to atone for our regrets.

September 20, 1994

Regulations Can't Be Abolished

Few of us like any regulation of our activities; we'd much prefer to be free of rules that interfere with the conduct of our lives. It's more pleasant to do as we please without having to suffer the limitations that society places on us.

Reasoning of that type must have prevailed in biblical times, when life was simpler and less complicated than it is today. Yet even then, with a smaller known world, without the complexities of 20th-century industrial life, without television and radio, the Jewish religious leaders decided that an unregulated society was leading its people into disaster, that rules of conduct and human relationship had to be codified and taught to the rank and file.

The chore of writing the laws of human conduct, better known to us as the Ten Commandments, must have been much like writing a contemporary political platform. Different groups wanting to cover a wide variety of rules had to compromise and accept one delegate's commandment in exchange for the inclusion of a favorite one of another's.

When it was all finished, the committee's report was conveyed to Moses, who brought down from Mount Sinai the laws, which were incorporated in the Bible as holy writ. Other religions encountered the same needs, and each in its own way created documents that set forth similar limitations on human conduct. All of them are similar in general concept.

There must have been opponents to these laws then, just as there are opponents to regulations today. In an ideal world, populated only by ideal people, regulations of both personal and business conduct wouldn't be necessary. Unfortunately, all people and all business enterprises are not equally honest, altruistic and responsible.

With human nature being what it is, there are wide ranges of interpretation of honesty among individuals, selfish motivations, due to the heritage of mankind's evolutionary development in which self-protection and self-interest were the motivating forces leading to individual survival.

As civilization progressed and humans banded together in primitive societies, rules began to evolve that limited the individual's power.

Shifting focus from primitive and biblical times to the 20th century, we find that mankind as a whole is no more honest, nor less selfish, nor more altruistic than its forebears were. As industry becomes worldwide in scope, life becomes even more complicated, and the need for rules and regulations becomes more vital for the security of all.

This is in no way a defense of regulation for the sake of regulation; it is by no means an attempt to label all regulations as good or even necessary. The fact, though, that we have had some bad regulations is not a valid reason to condemn all regulations, as some industrial leaders and ultraconservatives would lead us to believe.

Even the most rugged individuals would be unlikely to opt for the elimination of regulations testing the security of elevators, or for the safety inspections of aircraft or ocean liners. Nor would they choose to void the rules requiring financial institutions to protect the deposits of their customers, or the anti-tampering laws that appertain to the selection and protection of juries.

Yet we hear complaints constantly that government regulations interfere with business and prevent profit achievement. They who have been responsible for the blight that environmental abuse causes resent regulations that require them to pay for their own pollution. In a desperate effort to appease a few industries, the president ordered a temporary suspension of regulation enforcement to help stimulate economic recovery. That is not unlike the abandonment of the use of lifeboats for ten hours because the ship is sinking.

144

Until the millennium, mankind has no choice but to recognize the need for regulations, but it has the obligation to insist on good regulations, honestly administered.

February 18, 1992

ﻋﻢ

We Need to Be Reminded of Rules

At one time or another, everyone yearns for the undisciplined life—the ability to do what we want without restraints, either physical or mental, and on our own time schedules. That, of course, leads to license and then to anarchy and a destructive state of mind.

We all need discipline, and the best kind is that which is self-imposed. Every vocation from household work to legal practice to cooking to writing requires an individual willingness to set strict rules for self-conduct. Those who are self-disciplined find it easier to achieve objectives and to adjust to others in today's complex world. They tend to be happier and better adjusted to their peers.

Recognizing that all individuals don't march to the same drummer, society finds it necessary to supply some disciplinary memory jolts. Reminders like street-crossing markings reiterate the rules for the protection of pedestrians from vehicular traffic. Repetitive speed limit signs are necessitated, in part, by the wide variations of maximum limits in different blocks of the same street.

There are scores of other reminders, such as recorded messages on subways that remind embarking passengers to permit exiting riders time to get off the trains before they board. There also are bells that ring in many automobiles to indicate that the driver is exceeding the speed limit.

So all of us, disciplined and undisciplined, need reminders to observe society's rules. When those warnings fail to accomplish results, the next step is to establish laws with punishment for the offenders. Depending on the seriousness of the infraction, punishment may vary from the monetary fine to imprisonment.

As a matter of fact, biblical leaders found the need for a rule book of ethical standards to teach their people. As a result, the Ten Commandments were handed to Moses to help establish discipline in his society. It is obvious that he had many of the same problems we face, for a number of the commandments eventually were made into legal statutes. Nearly every religion has developed a set of principles of conduct similar to the Ten Commandments and has encountered the same problems that led to the need for legal enforcement.

A visitor from New York initiated this discussion the other night when, with fresh eyes, he observed that many street-crossing signs in Dallas had all but faded out and that speeding signs were missing due, in all probability, to the zealousness of a municipal budgeter who figured several thousand dollars could be saved every year by not repainting the zone warnings or replacing purloined signs.

He probably was correct in his judgment, but he failed to realize that we probably lost a half-dozen citizens in the process.

April 22, 1997

You Have to Be Ready for Retirement

One of the most touching admissions I have read was in a *Fortune* magazine interview with former Chrysler chairman Lee Iacocca. The title of the article on retired executives was "How I Flunked Retirement Twice." One of America's leading industrialists admitted he had developed no hobbies or interests that could provide amusement or a sense of purpose when he left his successful business career and entered the world of retirement.

Mr. Iacocca's experience isn't unlike those of other men who have been so engaged in making money that they haven't taken the time to develop hobbies or other leisure activities that could enrich their lives.

Some men learn about art, music, handcrafts and a score of other subjects. They didn't have to borrow too much time from their businesses, but they made the most of their uncommitted time to broaden their knowledge. It is remarkable what a person can learn in as short a period as an hour in a museum, bookstore or art gallery or with someone who is an authority on a subject.

When they were young, many men collected wide varieties of objects, from rocks and match covers to marbles and baseball cards. Those aren't exactly activities for adults, but getting into the habit of collecting makes a lasting impression.

Collecting gives one a sense of purpose when traveling. It is much more fun to go into a bookshop when in search of a rare edition of a biography that has been out of print for years. This is the way many men and women enhance their knowledge and get an extra dividend from life. Such individuals never flunk retirement, for they have prepared for it.

Mr. Iacocca ended his magazine interview with this: "You can plan everything in life, and the roof caves in on you because you haven't done enough thinking about who you are and what you should do with the rest of your life. Those guys who retire at 53 with early buyouts have a hell of a problem.

"Actuarially, I've got ten years left. I hope to beat it and do twenty. I'm here by myself now but still optimistic. People ask me why I'm still working so hard. I tell them that without that, and without my kids and grandkids, I'd lose it—I'd have nothing."

It takes a very astute person to be able to see himself with such objectivity. It happens only when the individual feels he has some good advice that might benefit others.

February 5, 1998

*S*ELF-KNOWLEDGE

We're All Like Don Quixote

Aristotle advised us to know ourselves, but any of us who have lived long enough to appreciate Aristotle understand we are many selves, and that we are different selves to different people.

Knowing ourselves is perhaps the most challenging of all tasks. It's both difficult to recognize our different selves and to admit they exist. Some of our selves we would prefer to deny, to be left incognito.

I was interviewed for a magazine profile the other day by a young reporter. Toward the end of the two hours I spent with him, he said, "My editor told me to find out what makes you tick. What makes you tick?"

Well, I've been a veteran of magazine profiles longer than that man has lived, so I was able to give him an answer that satisfied him, and will probably satisfy his editor, but it seems to me the answer should have come from the reporter, not the subject. We are the last people who know what makes us tick. We have a suspicion of what we are, but most of us don't have the courage to dig in and take charge of finding out, so we go through life living with a superficial knowledge of ourselves.

We are all a lot like Don Quixote, the mad Spanish gentleman who, besotted with his books about the glories of chivalry, believed himself to be a knight errant. He saw giants in windmills, armies in herds of sheep and queenly beauty in a rustic servant girl.

If you asked Quixote what made him tick, he'd answer without hesitation that it was his sense of duty as a knight. If you asked his friends, they'd say just as quickly it was insanity, that poor Quixote was mad as a March hare. The truth was *both* made Quixote tick:

chivalry and madness. We are all such a combination, a portion of what we think we are and a portion of what others think we are.

Perhaps one definition of self knowledge is our ability to understand which is which and to blend the two into a workable whole. I suspect that if Quixote had had a sudden revelation of self-awareness, he might have gone right ahead with tilting at windmills, recognizing it was a lot more fun than sitting around watching life pass him by.

If there's a constant "tick" to my life, it's the same as Quixote's, the desire to be an active participant in life, not just a spectator, even if it requires taking risks and sometimes looking foolish.
April 9, 1991

ૐ

Seeing Ourselves as Others See Us

"Oh wad some power the giftie gie us. To see ourselves as others see us!" When Robert Burns, the 18th-century Scots poet, wrote these lines, he didn't know we'd have that potentiality now. But it hasn't changed adults very much for the better, and it may have caused irreparable damage to our children.

In his charming poem "To a Louse," in which the above-mentioned quotation appears, Mr. Burns described how a proud, haughty woman at church was sure she was the subject of every admiring eye. Actually, members of the congregation were fascinated by a louse crawling up and down her bonnet strings. Her false pride would collapse into a more becoming humility, Mr. Burns believed, if she could only see herself as others did. I wonder what Mr. Burns would have thought about television?

One of the ironies of our human condition is that those of us who know ourselves literally from the inside out have no external perspective on ourselves as separate, physical beings. Locked behind our eyes, we can't help but see others more clearly than ourselves, but through the magic of electronics, television shows us as living, moving beings. Thanks to the increase in local programming brought about by cable and local-access channels, more of us will have the opportunity to see ourselves as others see us.

The result, however, if my experience and those to whom I've talked holds true, will not be massive self-improvement, but massive disbelief. Friends who have seen themselves on television once or twice tell me they feel a sense of unreality when they look at their onscreen selves. I've been on television frequently enough over the years to have come to accept the notion that the vaguely familiar looking fellow with the beard is indeed me, but still have a split-second "Who's that?" feeling. Why is it that our first impression of our television image is likely to be, "Where have I seen him before?"

There is some doubt as to whether we really do want to see ourselves as others see us. It's a rare individual who can take that kind of introspection. Many who have tried it have been so shocked that they ended up on the psychiatric couch. I think most of us are more satisfied with the illusion or delusion of what and who we are. This conclusion may not be true in the case of actors and actresses in motion pictures and TV, who get to see themselves over and over again. I would presume that the more astute performers would choose to study themselves on film and tape to get a better understanding of their strengths and weaknesses. Certainly politicians have benefited from hearing and seeing their speeches played back to them.

It's possible that our suspicions of our television images may indicate that Mr. Burns' wish will never be answered. Survival of our egos, if not our species, may depend on built-in blinders that shield us from the complete, unvarnished truth about ourselves. July 28, 1992

If Customer Isn't Right, Pretend

In the question-and-answer session that followed a speech I had given, a member of the audience asked what I had found to be the best way of dealing with unfair customer demands. I told him that I believed most customers were honest. Some might be wrong in what they expected out of a product, but they at least had the conviction they were right.

He told me that his problem had to do mainly with customers who made complaints after the warranty expired, when the manufacturer assumed no responsibility. I advised him that you make friends out of customers more with honey than with vinegar.

If I felt the customer believed he had a grievance, warranty or not, I would try to meet his demands. Besides, the customer was not doing business with the manufacturer but with the merchant, and he had every reason to look to the merchant for satisfaction.

I asked the young businessman how much those claims totaled. About $500 each, he told me. I then asked how many claims he encountered in a year. About a dozen, he replied. I said, "Well, we now can put a dollar value on those unfair requests—about $6,000."

I inquired how much a full-page color ad would cost in a regional magazine. About $6,000, he told me. I said, "In that case, I would recommend that you drop one of the ads from your schedule and use that money to give complete customer satisfaction. Be sure you do it gracefully, after explaining that you are willing to assume the responsibility."

"If you adopt this policy," I told him, "you will enjoy life more, your sales staff will have renewed confidence in you, your actions will be the topic of dinner conversation all over the city, and, best of all, you will reduce the likelihood of developing high blood pressure and ulcers. All the way around, you win, when you sell satisfaction rather than just merchandise.

"Once you have made up your mind to follow this philosophy, you should stop worrying and simply enjoy the knowledge that you have gone beyond the call of duty to make a satisfied customer." I said he would be surprised at how quickly irate customers could be converted to enthusiasts.

Several months later, the businessman called to tell me that he had tried my suggestion and that one irate customer, so pleased by the merchant's willingness to satisfy, had sent his two sons to the store two months later to be totally outfitted. I told him that I was surprised it had taken so long.

The great merchant John Wannamaker was right when he said, "The customers are not always right, but it is better business to pretend that they are."

May 11, 1993

ᓫ

Making Peace Can Carry a Low Price

Shortly after World War II, a brilliant young fashion creator for Metro-Goldwyn-Mayer decided to offer his clothes to the public through a limited number of prestige stores. His clothes were very dramatic and striking, but also very expensive. His name was Gilbert Adrian, but his signature was his last name. One day, a wealthy customer complained to me about a $7,500 beaded evening gown Adrian had designed.

The customer opened the conversation by saying, "This is the most beautiful dress I've ever seen, but the price is outrageous." I agreed with her on both counts and told her, "You look superb in that dress, which appears as though it might have been custom made for you. I agree about the price; it's exorbitant, and I told

153

Adrian that it was far too expensive. He told me that it took three seamstresses three weeks to embroider all the beads that covered the dress. 'I'll give you the dress and beads if you will put them on,' he said. I politely declined the offer, but it was so beautiful that I couldn't leave it behind."

That answer didn't satisfy her. "You know I've been doing business with you for many years, and this is the first time I have ever asked you to change your price." "Yes," I replied, "you've been a very faithful customer, and you've been shopping with us long enough to know that we have one price, and that's the price on the ticket." She replied, "I'm going to Paris tomorrow, and if you mark it down to $5,000, I'll take it. No one will ever know about it." I replied, "When clearance time comes, the price will be changed publicly. The first customer who comes in can buy it at the new price."

Still protesting, she said, "You are making a mistake. No one will ever pay $7,500 for this dress." As a final word, she said, "I'll bet you $100 that you don't get the $7,500, but if you do, you'll have to agree to tell me who the darn fool was who bought it." I accepted her challenge.

The customer went on to Europe, and I forgot about the transaction until a few days later. The sales directress of the couture department told me, "Last evening, a man came in and bought the Adrian dress that you were showing Mrs. Smith." "Who was the purchaser?" I asked. With a twinkle in her eye, she replied, "It was Mr. Smith."

"Was he going to take the dress to Paris as a surprise for Mrs. Smith?" I asked. "No," she replied. "He was on his way to California." A month later when she returned, Mrs. Smith visited the store and asked to see the dress. When she found out it had been sold, she called for me and asked whether the dress was still available. I was in a jam. I could not disclose the purchaser, so I reached in my pocket, pulled out a $100 bill and said, "Mrs. Smith, your judgment was better than mine. The dress did not sell until our fall clearance started, and then it sold at a reduced price. You win your bet."

154

A dozen years later, I picked up an out-of-town newspaper and read the account of the fiftieth wedding anniversary of Mr. and Mrs. Z. F. Smith (not their real names), and I recognized that the price of my silence was golden.

July 23, 1993

૪**

"Don't Thread on Me!"

Benjamin Franklin had a knack for summarizing bits of wisdom in brief and pithy sentences. He surveyed life constantly and evidenced no reluctance to epitomize his conclusions.

In his *Maxims Prefixed to Poor Richard's Almanac*, he wrote: "A little neglect may breed mischief; for want of a nail the shoe was lost; for want of a shoe the horse was lost; and for want of a horse the rider was lost."

The fact that this old folk story wasn't original didn't bother him. He took a bit of phrasing from a poem by George Herbert, a British poet of the preceding century, and added a beginning sentence that made the quotation applicable to the late 18th century.

I would like to revise these words to fit a contemporary situation that might read: "For want of a thread a button was lost; for want of a button a shirt was lost; and for want of a shirt a sunscreen was lost."

This relates to one of the failures of present-day garment manufacturing.

We have brought mass production to such sophistication that we can design clothes in Paris or New York, cut the patterns made by elaborate blueprint machines, fax them to Korea, Sri Lanka and Turkey, sew them, press them and pack them to be shipped by air to Western markets with amazing coordination and speed.

But the one thing the trade has failed to do is to examine these garments, despite well-touted quality control programs, and to delegate the responsibility of clipping the myriad threads whose loose ends form a virtual fringe on skirts, blouses, shirts and pajamas.

Lest I put the blame on mass-production workers, the lack of production discipline shows up not only in domestic factory-made products but also in custom-made shirts from England, costly bedsheets from Italy and expensive fur coats made in this country. The other day, I clipped seventeen stray threads from a new, unlaundered, made-to-order shirt from a renowned Jermyn Street shirtmaker.

The fact that loose threads bother me is of no importance. What is significant is the message that loose threads send. They are saying, "We are here because the maker of this product doesn't care about going all the way to provide you with a garment free of loose threads."

This represents a triumph for slipshod production techniques, which, like the germs from a common cold, can spread to one and all producers of autos, coffee roasters, planes and roller coasters. Sad to say, most retailers fail to guard against such sloppy product inspection.

This is an unhappy epitaph for the end of the 20th century, when we have seen numerous superb achievements.

May 9, 1995

 ❧

Retailers Don't Provide Free Lunch

It appears that the days are gone when a product or service is sold on the pure merits of its quality. In today's oversaturated consumer goods market, all sorts of schemes are spawned by ambitious merchants to reward purchasers with bonuses of one type or another.

I guess it all started thirty years ago, when a vigorous new purveyor in the cosmetics field bullied her way into the realm of

156

customer recognition by offering a "gift with purchase." This innocuous phrase revolutionized the cosmetics industry. The name of the newcomer was Estee Lauder, who vigorously pushed her way into competition with the reigning beauty gurus, Elizabeth Arden and Helena Rubinstein.

"Gift with purchase" became a standard in the routine of cosmetic sales promotion. Not only were items from the maker's inventory used as gifts, but such totally unrelated objects as umbrellas and cameras became the rewards as well.

This practice has become so successful in stimulating business that it has spread in diversified forms to the automobile trade, real estate, the hotel industry and others selling direct to consumers. Just this month, the venerable Plaza Hotel in New York City offered a free Mikimoto cultured pearl necklace to guests who stayed at the Plaza for two nights.

It has gotten so only a fool or a stranger from Mars is willing to buy anything unless there is a bonus attached to the purchase.

This, of course, is symptomatic of a buyer's market. In order to move goods, either price concessions must be made to bring buyers into the market, or inducements of one type or another are brought into play to accomplish the same result.

There is nothing new about the technique. Anyone old enough may recall the days when free china was a feature of soap sales in the grocery stores or when baseball bats were given away at the games of slumping baseball teams. This is the free market's way of temporarily stimulating demand to absorb an oversupply of stock. Today, American Airlines practices this with its highly successful AAdvantage program, as do a host of emulators.

While the process can be conceived as a means of buying customers' loyalty in an economy that is so highly oversupplied, it must be discouraging to a craftsman whose product was his best advertisement. Today, the only sure thing is that the buyer is on a free-gift hunt and often takes second best to get a premium.

The next time you are tempted, take an extra moment to evaluate the bargain you are getting. Is it truly a "gift," or are you sacrificing quality when you get two for the price of one?

As King Solomon must have learned a few thousand years ago, "There is no such thing as a free lunch."

December 5, 1995

Poor Service Undercuts the Economy

Customer service is closely related to profitability in every type of business—large or small. That fact is so obvious, it shouldn't require constant reiteration.

Common sense should be a reminder that bad customer service, or even mediocre service, results in dampening the customer's desire to buy, whether it be the purchase of a book or a ton of steel.

I haven't been in the market for a ton of steel in a long time, but I am a frequent book buyer. Last week in Santa Fe, I was attempting to locate a particular book as a gift to an artist friend. I phoned one museum that had a shop that concentrated on folk-art books.

A salesman advised me that he didn't think the shop carried the title. I asked if he would take a look at the bookshelves to verify his opinion. He returned to the phone in a minute and triumphantly proclaimed that his impression was correct. However, he did advise me to call the shop of another museum, which he explained "carried a larger stock." I followed his advice and spoke to a woman at the second museum. I received a polite but negative reply.

Finally, on phoning an independent bookstore, I was greeted by a saleswoman who showed a genuine interest in my inquiry. She said, "I don't think we carry this book, but let me check to be sure."

In about thirty seconds, she was back to me. Although the shop didn't have the book, she said she would be pleased to order it and assured me that it would be delivered within a week. She even told me the name of the publisher and the prices for both the hardback and softcover editions. With delight, I accepted her offer, and she made a $40 sale.

Note that the first two sellers I contacted made little effort to suggest other books that might have been adequate substitutes, nor did either of them offer to order the title I wanted.

The economy isn't going to topple as a result of two successive failures to make a sale, nor will the production charts reflect the success of the person who did make the sale. But lost sales can add up.

Although there are no statistics available to indicate the total number, let's say similar incidents happen five million times a year. With a $40 average sale, that comes to $200 million.

In my illustration, the sale *was* made. But very often, sales simply evaporate, for many buyers find other solutions, including the one of deciding not to make any purchase.

The ultimate loss to individual institutions can be staggering. Bad service, or disinterested service, turns customers away as surely as a sign on the door that says, "We aren't interested in selling to you."
June 4, 1996

ॐ

Good Service Starts at the Top

Service—or the lack of it—is one of the most common topics of conversation. It is second only to the weather and traffic. The mere mention of the word releases a flood of horror stories about what may have occurred at a supermarket checkout counter, shoe store or neighborhood bistro.

The problem about customer service is that it is easier to discuss than to improve. There are at least three basic approaches to actually improving service.

The first is by mandate of an employer or supervisor. That involves making a rule that will be enforced by a prescribed schedule of penalties, followed by employment termination for noncompliance. Such an approach requires stern enforcement procedures that may produce a grim administrative attitude and at best can produce only perfunctory compliance. Dictated service always looks cold, for it lacks human kindness as its motive.

The second approach is designed to educate employees about the virtues of good service and begins with the selection of job applicants who are encouraged to understand from the beginning that superior customer service is part of the job. The personnel manager selects those who appear to be most likely to support the service standards of the company and who are willing to participate in the program without reluctance. This is the plan most used by the majority of companies that recognize that the responsibility to render good service at all levels is an integral part of their operating policy.

The third approach is based on a genuine desire to be helpful to customers, whatever they may purchase. This will wash only when the management of the organization has such a deep commitment to a sincere standard of service that sales and supportive staffs accept the program with full commitment and enthusiasm.

When employees recognize that a boss's objectives are genuine and consistent, it doesn't take long for them to back him up with full enthusiasm and excitement. The greater the firm's reputation for service grows, the larger are the number of employees who become participants. Pride for giving good service becomes a matter of second nature.

Spontaneous service brings joy to both receiver and giver. It is an exhilarating experience to be part of a group that genuinely enjoys doing things for other people.

These generalizations about customer service apply to all types of business groups, ranging from doctors' officers to stores to hospitals to theaters to restaurants to municipal offices.

Good management gives proper recognition and rewards to those who provide good service. It becomes a company goal to do so, and individual staff members help educate their co-workers. It can be done. It has been done. It needs to be done more.

Good customer service has to come from people who like people and enjoy being nice to them. It doesn't come in jars or tubes; it only can come from the heart.

January 13, 1998

HOPPING

Anything Can Be Made Better

In my quest for the best, I've always thought that olive oil, particularly that labeled "virgin," was the best. Recently, I've found that there's a grade higher with which I was not familiar.

One of the exciting things about shopping is that if you're persistent and perceptive, you're likely to find something that is better than anything you had previously imagined. This was a discovery I made years ago when I was commissioning a fur manufacturer to make a mink coat for one of my most demanding customers. After selecting the skins, I asked the manufacturer whether this would be the finest mink coat that money could buy.

He replied, "No, you can always make it finer."

I asked, "How come? I'm paying you an arm and a leg for this coat, and now you tell me it won't be the best."

He went on to say, "It's always possible to make something finer. If I cut off a little bit more of the bellies and used more backs, that could make the coat finer. If I waited another year, I could probably improve the matching of the skins. If I waited two to three years, I could make even finer matches. But by the time I waited for the ultimate match, your customer may have died. There's no limit to perfection."

Coming back to the olive oil I mentioned, I was in a fine epicure shop recently, and I came upon a bottle of olive oil that was marked "extra virgin olive oil." The label went on to explain that this oil had been put through a distilling process twice as long as that of the more ordinary virgin olive oil, and the price was just about double.

162

"The proof is in the eating," and after I had finished my salad, the dressing for which had been made with the extra virgin oil, I had to concur that it was a superior gustatory experience. It may not be that I would want to eat it with every meal, but two or three times a week would titillate any palate. I recommend a dollop in an Italian white bean soup or poured on a plate of toasted bread with ground pepper, or on fresh sliced tomatoes or fennels.

I hadn't realized that virginity came in several degrees, but the extra virgin oil I've just described did have a better flavor and less aftertaste than the ordinary virgin oil. It was worth the price, not only for the taste, but to learn that there was something better than simple virgin oil.

Similar experiences await careful and discriminating shoppers who will eventually come up with the best of anything and everything.

Don't settle for less than the best. It's a wonderful challenge.
March 27, 1990

❧

Only Thirty-Six Shopping Days Till Christmas!

The great avalanche of Christmas shopping is about to slide down on retailers, most of whom will be well organized and stocked to serve the gift demands of their customers.

In view of the fact that the November-to-December business in stores constitutes 25 percent of their annual volume and 33 percent of their profits, it is important that retailers try to make Christmas shopping a memorable event.

Dallas is one of the top shopping markets in the country, with a wide variety of department and specialty stores, as well as a vast assortment of category and specialized shops in the suburbs.

If a shopper knows where to look, there is virtually nothing that can't be found in the Dallas area. Knowing where to look gives a buyer an edge on friends who may not have done as good a scouting job.

In my retailing days, I used to watch customers as they made their Christmas gift selections. Many of them failed to systematize their shopping, while others made it easier on themselves and those who served them.

The best-prepared shoppers arrived in the store with an alphabetized Christmas shopping list. They even presented the salesperson with a slip of paper on which the name, address and ZIP code of the recipient was typed, together with a gift card. They then noted their purchases in their shopping book.

Before they arrived, they had recorded their previous year's gift to each recipient and the price ranges they favored. That information had been codified by floors, so they didn't waste time going back and forth between the various floors. Above all, they knew what size shirt Uncle Tom wore and the ages and sizes of their nieces and great-grandchildren.

Customers who are so well prepared find that they can complete their gift shopping in half the time. That foresight gives them three or four extra days to enjoy the pleasant diversions of a holiday season.

Another tip: Come early in the morning, when both you and the salespeople are fresh. Lots of customers never have learned that.

The single most frequent mistake I have observed is that many shoppers buy a gift that meets their price objective but not the recipient's taste. It is better to buy the best of one category than to compromise on the poorest of another. If the best shirt is too expensive for the budget, then shift to the best pair of socks or the best belt. That practice helps maintain the budget, and it makes a world of difference to those who are on the receiving end.

Many sophisticated Christmas shoppers don't even shop in December. They start their search in January for the following Christmas. They take advantage of the clearances to pick up real bargains, and they continue to buy throughout the summer as they come across appropriate gifts. By September, they are finished and go off on a late fall trip without nagging thoughts of what they have to do on their return.

There is an old Chinese proverb that goes, "If you buy the best, you cry only once."

Happy shopping! It is later than you may think!

November 19, 1996

Sports Arenas Don't Have to Be Throwbacks

After all the local turmoil about athletic arenas, it was interesting to read about a new football stadium at Princeton University, which, incidentally, received a rave review. More about this in a few paragraphs.

The most recent disappointment about the Dallas arena has been the decision by the sports teams to speed up the architectural selection by choosing David Schwarz, who did The Ballpark at Arlington and the Bass Performance Hall in Fort Worth. The choice, which was the teams' right to exercise, met with mixed reviews, including very strong criticism from the architectural community. Even louder dissent came from a number of architectural buffs with no connection, past or present, to the building trades or designers.

The whole manner in which the site selection and architectural choice were handled has left a bad impression in the community. The approval of a design style reminiscent of the 1930s is one that the teams will have to live with. Possibly, the best thing they can do will be to shroud it behind a heavy screen of large trees.

It was nice to read that Princeton was able to build a 30,000-seat stadium and score an international best for the beauty of the work. Herbert Muschamp, writing in the *New York Times*, describes the architect, Rafael Vinoly, as "the most elegant architect now practicing in the United States." He goes on to comment that "in the last decade, with places like Denver Coors Field, the sports stadium has emerged as America's most diseased (public) building type."

The Dallas sports teams have made their decision, and nothing tangible can be changed. But the value of reopening the subject is in itself an educational matter.

Other important public buildings for sports, theater, music, and ballet will be built, and it can only be hoped that this recent controversy will have educated a larger segment of the public to expect and demand higher aesthetic values in the structures. As more and more public voices are heard, city managers and mayors will be more responsive to their responsibility in safeguarding the aesthetic reputation of Dallas.

Financial progressiveness is a common characteristic of the great cities of the world. Along with that quality is the other side of the coin—the aesthetic expression given by the buildings and facilities that line our streets. Pioneers first built exteriors worthy of their times; they didn't pay too much attention to the interior. As time went on, they learned that if they built interiors as attractive as the exteriors, they attracted more tenants and received more income from their investments.

Cities like Paris, Florence and Madrid all learned those lessons and, as a result, became the goals for all travelers to visit.

Not only is a beautiful and harmonious city good for tourists, but of equal importance, it is good for those who have to look at it every day.

September 1, 1998

ᔐ

Olympics Not an Unmixed Blessing

The initial conversations about the idea of Dallas hosting the 2012 Summer Olympics sound like the comments that were made in the *Atlanta Journal-Constitution* in the years prior to that city's successful quest for the 1996 Games.

A new cause can stimulate a lot of people to action if it is something that particularly interests them and if it offers the early comers a chance to become major participants.

A decision on the host city for the 2012 Games is a long way off, for there will be a sustained period of horse trading between the Olympic Committee and the cities competing for the Games. The committee fully recognizes the value of the attraction it controls and is committed to producing a contract with the biggest financial package.

Most of us who have lived through all sorts of promotional events know that very costly extravaganzas, which bring hundreds of thousands of guests, rarely produce the financial benefits projected in the initial discussions.

Events like the Olympics, major political party conventions or large sports events seldom live up to forecasts of volume and profitability. The benefits are reflected in higher occupancy rates for hotels and increased sales for restaurants. But the benefits don't support the high costs of staging the events. The truth of the matter is that such gatherings have so many programs of interest that the visitors have little interest in other civic attractions.

In Atlanta, many residents decided to get out of town during the Games to take vacations. They received healthy rentals for their homes but left an empty city behind them. It was commonplace to hear from visitors that many of their friends were away from the city during July and August.

The real value, possibly the only one to hold up under objective scrutiny, is the effect the Olympic Games would have on general cleanup programs. The city would be forced to engage in a gigantic renewal effort in all areas, for the intense spotlight focused on Dallas would pick up every blemish.

The city administration would be so afraid that the city would be criticized for potholes, unmowed lawns and derelict houses that a good housekeeping program would be inaugurated and maintained for the duration of the Games, after which things could revert to normal very quickly.

Still, the cleanup would be an important achievement.

Who would be the major beneficiaries? Hotels obviously do very well when they are able to get 100 percent occupancy during the hot summer months. So would popularly priced restaurants, mass transit and parking lots in the vicinity of the Games' event sites. Major benefits also would go to individuals who worked their hearts out to get everything ready and to whoever was mayor at that time. But the Games would come at the cost of a lot of headaches for local residents who would be made uncomfortable.

I kid thee not.

September 15, 1998

ALENT

The Unrecognized Talent

At one time or another, most of us feel as if the world doesn't recognize our talent, but that's no reason to worry. The world is often a little nearsighted.

A *New York Times* story not long ago gives hope to all the unrecognized writers and painters and designers and just about anyone else who hasn't received his just rewards.

A California prankster sent the original screenplay of *Casablanca* to 217 agents. He changed the title and the name of one character, Sam, the piano player, and only 33 agents recognized the movie. The other 184 turned it down.

And what did those imperceptive, even insensitive critics say was wrong with the script? One reader said it was too wordy. He thought lines like "You wore blue; the Germans wore gray" were unnecessary. He noticed too many repetitions of the phrase, "Here's looking at you, kid." He also suggested getting rid of the phrase, "All the gin joints in the world, and she had to come into mine."

Of course, some of the readers were a little more hopeful, like the one who said, "If Angie Dickinson says she'll do it, we'll be glad to think about it." Who, I wonder, would they suggest for the part Humphrey Bogart played? Sylvester Stallone, maybe?

Let's face it, all ideas aren't necessarily good. As a matter of fact, I would venture the guess that most new ideas aren't good. They're good in the minds of the originators, they are wonderful in the opinion of fond mothers, but in the marketplace, they may lack substance, originality or practicality. Sometimes they are just plain silly. I speak from experience, having come up with ideas that fit all of the above-mentioned descriptions.

Not even all good ideas find a home. Many are stillborn and never see the light of day. This is unfortunate, but that's the way it is. The one thing that an individual with an idea can do is to persevere, trying different methods to attract attention. Sometimes an idea is ahead of its time. Other times it needs to be exposed to another group of people with different standards and criteria. Many ideas are saved when the originator is savvy enough to accept and use sound criticism.

It takes courage and conviction to keep the chin up in face of negative reactions, but frequently the difference between talent that's rewarded and talent that's not is simply a talent for sticking it out.

June 31, 1988

Taste Now Is Everybody's Business

Taste, good or bad, always exists, but it is never static or permanent. Taste that may be good to one generation is likely to seem bad to the next.

In my book *Quest for the Best*, I described "taste" in these words: "There are different kinds of taste—taste in food, which is related to the physical senses; taste in manners, which is associated with the mores of the time; and aesthetic taste, which has to do with the selection of objects, colors, proportion of forms, and the harmonious arrangement and use of them. Regardless of which taste we may be talking about, 'good' taste has as its prerequisite the elements of discrimination, knowledge and experience."

At best, taste is a matter of opinion subject to changing times and fluctuating evaluations. Each person is entitled to his own taste opinion, but some more so than others. There's bad taste, good taste and superb taste. There is insecure taste and sure taste. There's conservative taste and garish taste.

Some individuals tend to overrate the quality of their own taste, and they take offense when it's questioned. Others who are unsure of their taste mask their insecurity by purchasing articles with designer labels. Many a fight has occurred over challenges to another's taste. It is prudent to accept the Latin phrase *De gustibus non est disputandum* ("There is no disputing about taste"). And, as the late James Laver, the British fashion historian, wrote, "Few of us would be willing to admit without argument that another man's taste is as good as ours."

The most melancholy task I've ever performed was to tell a store buyer that she had bad taste. Such an accusation cuts to the quick as no other that I can recall, other than advising that a person's breath is bad. People will accept all other types of criticism with equanimity and even appreciation, but not those relating to taste and breath.

Good taste, I'm convinced, can be acquired through environment and education; the eye can be educated to differentiate between good and bad by the process of constant looking. Any person with a normal IQ who is not colorblind can develop good taste. The achievement of superb taste is as difficult as the attainment of perfection in any endeavor. Taste was once the prerogative of the rich, but with the development of mass production, mass consumption and mass communication, taste became everybody's business.

Today, the amount of taste information that is disseminated through advertising, news stories in the daily press and magazines, on TV, and in movies exposes everybody to so much criteria on taste that it seems impossible for people to have a lack of awareness on the subject. Yet they do. Some people are impervious to good taste; they have their own taste and are determined to stick to it.

Many others, though, take advantage of the opportunity to improve their taste by study, comparative shopping, visits to museums and exhibitions. A wise person, interested in the subject, should seek a good critic who can help clarify some of the contradictions in taste. It is reported that Pierre Renoir said to his fellow painter, Paul Cezanne, "How can you wear that cravat? Can't you see it's in bad taste?" To which Mr. Cezanne reputedly replied, "If it were in bad taste, I wouldn't be wearing it."
March 20, 1990

૯ৡ৴

174

Expensive Tastes

There's an accepted adage that declares an expert is somebody from out of town. Faced with several out-of-towners, how do we determine who's the best? Do we usually assume it's the one who charges the most?

Freelance photography is one of those businesses wherein it's hard to make a living, particularly in a place as competitive as Houston, but one young photographer I knew there not only made a comfortable livelihood but supported a temperamental, yellow sports car and a playboy kind of lifestyle filled with women of demanding tastes. He openly boasted about the fact that he was the most expensive photographer in town.

That may have worked temporarily, but I do not believe that the public can be misled by unjustified high prices for any considerable period of time. Today's buyers of photography or furs or jewels or fresh produce are too well educated in comparative shopping to buy anything not competitively priced, all things considered.

In contradiction to my opinion, I came upon a survey of restaurants conducted by the *Wall Street Journal*. The writer suggested that the highest-priced items were the most popular. The fallacy of this finding may lie in the fact that the highest-priced items were dishes the public enjoyed eating more than those less costly. I'm confident that strawberries Romanoff is more expensive than stewed rhubarb.

Intangibles such as decor, the number and skill of waiters, menu variety and convenience of location contribute to both the cost and value of the services rendered.

People have been known to employ lawyers or doctors with reputations for being high-priced, but their decisions were doubtlessly motivated by word of mouth and by the practitioner's extraordinary skills and results. I seriously question if many people would deliberately search for the most expensive tax expert or dentist. I think they do look for the best, with a willingness to pay

175

the going price to those with outstanding reputations for performance.

From my experience as a retail merchant, I developed a healthy respect both for my customers, whose common sense was repelled by overpricing, and for my competitors, most of whom always sold their goods at prices justified by their standards of quality and customer service.

Only the gullible buyers (and there aren't too many of them) pay beyond the value they receive. A writer or politician might score quite a hit with a slogan like, "You can fool some of the people some of the time."

February 5, 1991

Simple Toasts Are Best Ones

At one time or another, most of us have been called upon to propose a toast. And most of us know that awful feeling of being tongue-tied, of not having a single appropriate thing to say.

According to Webster, a toast is made to "a person, thing, idea, etc., in honor of which a person or persons raise their glass and drink." But to many, a toast is when all eyes look to them to say something brilliant. Actually the best toasts are simple ones.

For example, if called upon to toast a fraternal organization, try this toast: "Here's to the land we love and the love we land." Ireland is also a source of many a fine toast, like this one: "May the flower of love never be nipped in the frost of disappointment, nor the shadow of grief fall among a member of this circle." And here is an old favorite: "May misfortune follow you all the days of your life and never overtake you."

Some of the best toasts are those that take their cue from previous toasts. There's a story, for example, about a dinner of foreign ministers after the American Revolutionary War. The British ambassador stood up and toasted, "To England—the sun whose bright beams enlighten and fructify the remotest corners of the world."

The French ambassador toasted, "To France—the moon, whose mild, steady and cheering rays are the delight of all nations, controlling them in the darkness and making their dreariness beautiful."

Benjamin Franklin, taking his cue from the two foreign ambassadors, toasted, "To George Washington—the Joshua who commanded the sun *and* moon to stand still, and they obeyed him."

One of the old-time favorite toasts is to the four sins:

"To lying—to protect a lady.

"To stealing—to steal away from bed.

"To drink—drink only in the best company.

"To gluttony—feast in the plums of our old friendships."

There is some confusion as to the proper time to propose a toast. Should it be at the moment when all the guests have been seated and the wine just poured? Or should it be immediately before or following dessert?

Both times are correct, but at a formal dinner, champagne is usually served with dessert. While the glasses are full and bubbling seems to many to be the appropriate time to toast the honored guests—brides and grooms, visitors from out of the city or from abroad.

The next time you are called on to give a toast, relax and speak from your heart. A fine toast improves the flavor of any drink, whether it's a scotch on the rocks or a lemonade.

September 10, 1985

A Fictitious Animal and a Beloved President

What toy is loved by children and adults alike, is named after one of our presidents and even resembles one? The other day I ran into a collection of teddy bears decorating the waiting room of an orthopedic surgeon, which prompted me to do a bit of research on the genesis of this fictitious animal.

You don't have to be an arctophile, or bear lover, to know that the answer is the teddy bear. Back in 1902, this lovable creature was named after the man whom Walter Lippmann, the distinguished columnist of the '50s, called our only "lovable" president, Theodore Roosevelt.

History has it that President Roosevelt was on a hunting trip. After many hours without sighting a single bear, his dogs cornered a limping cub. Luckless though his hunt had been, Mr. Roosevelt refused to shoot it.

The incident was memorialized by a popular political cartoonist of the day, and the country loved it! Soon there were "Roosevelt and the Bear" buttons, and pins, and mugs.

Then an enterprising candy store owner named Morris Michtom took it one step further. He asked Mr. Roosevelt for permission to name a small, stuffed bear after him. The president replied, "I doubt if my name will mean much in the bear business, but go ahead." And so the teddy bear was born.

Mr. Michtom went on to found one of America's largest toy companies. And that original teddy bear went on to sit in the Smithsonian Institution. Today, nearly eighty years later, the teddy bear is still king of the playroom. And more than that, it's a symbol of childhood on which many people like to hang their nostalgia.

As Peter Bull says in *The Teddy Bear Book*, "Teddy bears have saved lives by intercepting bullets, breaking falls, or just being around. They have flown around the world, been drowned in floods, burned in concentration camps and worshipped as totems. There are no cases of disloyal, treacherous or cowardly teddy bears."

For years now, the teddy bear has become a regular feature in many of the nation's Christmas catalogues. He has been dressed as a soccer player, a hunter, a soldier, and a sailor. He has been carried to bed and on transcontinental trips by both boys and girls as their most loyal and dependable link to society.

No other president has been successful in passing along a symbol of such universality. I seriously doubt that Teddy Roosevelt had any idea of what a gift he was making to the psyche of young and old Americans.

November 30, 1993

Seeing How Others Do Things

One of the major benefits of foreign travel is that it usually forces comparisons with practice and manners that we are accustomed to at home. Sometimes we find their methods are better than ours; in other cases we can take satisfaction in our superior solutions.

When we took our children to Europe for their first voyage overseas in the late '40s, I told them that the most important part of the trip was for them to compare the way things were done in Europe with the way we did them at home and to observe how the various national groups could do things differently from us and still be right.

This became an interesting game for them. Our daughters pointed out that the French held their knives and forks in variance from the manner they had been taught was correct, and our son noticed that the Belgians stacked hay in a completely different way than the farmers in central Texas. All three were startled by the fact that the English drove on the "wrong" side of the street but were never arrested for their error. The recognition that others can perform everyday activities in ways different than ours and still be just as right as we are is the beginning of wisdom.

Tolerance of those who are foreign to us and have different customs is essential to peaceful co-existence. This used to be something we realized only when we traveled abroad; now it is evident as people from Russia, Vietnam and South America settle on these shores and as our next-door neighbors.

The huge jump in foreign travel has enabled millions of American visitors and other travelers to this country to enlarge their food experiences and to develop international taste palates. One of the first and most important differences is in food and eating habits. Just as American food preferences such as hamburgers and hot dogs have found ready acceptance in foreign countries, so have pasta, egg rolls and enchiladas become very popular here.

Mexican cuisine has become the fastest-growing style of cooking in this country, closely followed by Italian and the numerous Asian cuisines. An examination of the shelves of any supermarket will give further evidence to the changes that have occurred.

Restaurants, as well as food retailers, are being forced not only to fill the demands of ethnic and nationalist groups for food familiar to them, but to meet the changing tastes of their native American patrons as well. Even the produce departments in the markets are responding to demand by providing fresh cilantro and peppers for Hispanic dishes and Chinese cabbage and snow peas for Oriental recipes.

Thanks to the public awareness of cholesterol and physical fitness and to the enlargement of our menus by the inclusion of foreign dishes, we shall no longer be a meat and potatoes society. June 30, 1992

❧

The Rewards of Living Abroad

Any travel broadens the mind, as the old saying goes, but to live and work for a year in another country must surely change our outlook forever—and for the better. We never see ourselves so clearly as when we look in the mirror of a foreign culture.

Living and working in another land brings out all sorts of problems and rewards as well. I have a granddaughter who is currently studying in Russia, where she has had a front-row seat at one of the most amazing political and economic spectacles of history.

She is learning much better than those of us at home how difficult it is to quickly substitute one economic system for another. She is experiencing the frustration of the Russian populace, and while she doesn't enjoy the slowness of daily accomplishment, she marvels at the patience of the Russian people.

A young friend who had just returned from a year in Brazil marveled at her discovery that our puritan work ethic does not exist there. Instead, she found Brazil's business climate to be relaxed and casual. She did the same type of job she held in the United States, yet her employer apologized for overworking her whenever her work load exceeded what she'd have considered to be a light day here.

Yet Brazil is a modern, industrialized country. Things get done and get done well. The difference is that we in this country make a virtue of working harder than necessary. This peculiar quirk in our nature is traceable to our Founding Fathers, who firmly believed that "idle hands are the Devil's workshop." It is reasonable and satisfying to work to live, but our forefathers taught us to live to work.

We gain our identity from our jobs. When we meet someone, we immediately follow "How do you do?" with "What do you do?" We grant the lowest status to those who don't work, a fact that would have brought millions of women from their home into the marketplace even if economic necessity hadn't. We even work hard at our play. We approve of vacations that involve sailing, skiing or hiking—anything that keeps us from the sin of doing nothing.

We can't even relax around the swimming pools we labored so hard to earn—we have to "work" on our tans.

This approach to living is not necessarily wrong. A lot of us thrive in the fast lane, and if we get more spiritual satisfaction from reaching the bottom of a pile of paperwork than from watching a sunset, our puritan forebears would beam with approval. Nonetheless, we must extend equal rights to those whose preference is to devote leisure time to the real pursuit of leisure.

All too often we fall into the trap of thinking that our attitudes are the "right" way to behave, since we accept them without considering their source. Life in another culture gives us an enlarged opportunity to understand and choose for ourselves.

July 7, 1992

ॐ

A Guide to Imaginary Places

The Dictionary of Imaginary Places is a book that describes magical lands as they are described in novels, stories, films, librettos, poems and plays. It appears to be a type of travel guide to many of the imaginary places in literature.

The book's dust jacket explains, "It explores geography, history, routes to take, and customs to follow, the language and characteristics of the inhabitants. Here are the words created to satisfy every desire for escape or perfection, dream kingdoms, and vampire cities, islands of terror where dark acts are practiced, intellectual curiosities and hilarious absurdities, architectural, musical, and permanent utopias, cities of impeccable virtue and unmitigated ire, cities that hang from the air or change at a glance." It was published by Macmillan in 1980 and may well be out of print by now.

Many of them are familiar, such as Sir Thomas More's *Utopia*, Samuel Butler's *Erewhon*, and the ones in Jonathan Swift's *Gulliver's Travels* and, of course, *The Prisoner of Zenda* by Anthony Hope, which tells the story of a fictional kingdom named Ruritania. It was this fantasy land that was the inspiration for a Neiman Marcus Fortnight in 1970, when a commitment from an actual foreign government fell through as a result of a change in administration.

The writers of those fantasies range from W. S. Gilbert and Arthur Sullivan, Lewis Carroll and C. S. Lewis to Carl Sandburg, Fyodor Dostoyevsky and Graham Greene.

184

For the past few weeks, I have been reading the travel advertisements in search of warmish places to visit during the cold winter months. I have been to a number of them, but they either have erratic weather, or they are not worth a return trip.

Many of the imaginary locations sound wonderful, better than even our most renowned resorts. Unfortunately, there is no air service at the present to any of them, with the exception of Epcot and Disney's Magic Kingdom in Orlando. The genius of Walt Disney and his dedicated successors has materialized many of the dream fantasies.

The public, American and foreign, has rewarded most of Disney's flights of imagination by enthusiastic patronage, with the exception of the new park outside of Paris. This appears to be the only place that Mickey Mouse and pals have stubbed their toes. Perhaps it was timing, or maybe the Disney leaders told the proud French what they were going to do, without pausing to listen to their reactions.

Success can lead to false assumptions, and perhaps Disney has had enough box office hits to make its corporate leaders inattentive to the discipline of listening.

All of this reminds me of a similar experience that the great Marks and Spencer retail operation of England had when it decided, a dozen years ago, to invade France with the stores that had been so successful throughout England. The venture was a flop; the French had different ideas about what they wanted to buy.

When a Marks and Spencer executive was asked how such a sophisticated management could have misjudged French tastes and markets before barging in, he replied, "Since France was just sixty miles away, we figured that Frenchmen would wear the same socks sold in the millions in our country, and that French women would like the same bras that pleased our most discriminating customers. But they didn't. We suffered from our own sheer arrogance; now we listen."

See Proverbs 16:18.

March 9, 1993

Umbrellas Always Get Last Laugh

Have you ever come in from the rain, soaking wet, and heard someone say, "You should have used an umbrella"?

The funny thing was, you *had* used one! First of all, you can be fairly sure that when you finally remember to carry your umbrella, it won't rain. An umbrella should be used as a safeguard against any possibility of rain.

Of course, there are days that start out pouring, so, naturally, you'll arm yourself with an umbrella. But think of the high expectations we have for these less-than-five-pound combinations of plastic and aluminum. Some rainy days are so windy that the battle becomes one with the umbrella. Your major struggle is trying to keep the tool over your head in its mushroom-like position. As the wind pulls your umbrella out of its protective shape, the problems are twofold: You get a little wet, but what's worse, you look a little foolish struggling in public with an inanimate object.

Those are some of the problems of the old-fashioned umbrella, but now a whole new set of conditions is triggered by that satanic invention, the automatic umbrella.

Unfortunately, windy days aren't the only days that cause so-called automatic umbrellas to rebel. They always have a way of opening up when we'd prefer they'd stay closed. Those newfangled, press-a-button umbrellas are terrific at this. True, these gadgets are great when you're in a downpour and have only one available hand, but given an accidental knock, they'll open on a crowded bus or subway.

One day in Paris, I was riding in one of those mini-cabs the French love, and my folding umbrella popped open, pinning me e back seat and effectively blocking both doors. When I reached my destination, I tried to explain my predicament, but the taxi driver—in his cynical, Gallic way—refused to help me. Momentarily, I could not think of the word for umbrella, which is *parapluie*, as everyone knows. Finally, in despair, I rallied my best French phrase and shouted, "Revenon au Hotel Ritz." On arrival, the ever-gracious doorman saw my plight, pressed the right button and restored me to freedom.

If you haven't made a public scene with your automatic umbrella, don't get too confident. It may refuse to open. It may pop open unexpectedly, or you'll probably forget about it altogether and leave it in a restaurant or taxi. Umbrellas always get the last laugh.

Now, I must admit that if there is a forecast for rain tomorrow, I'll still reach for my umbrella. However, I'll be prepared for more than rain!

May 3, 1988

Buildings Need Loving Parents, Too

In most cases, public buildings, such as city halls, court-houses, museums, symphony halls and memorial structures, are born with legal sanction and financing but shortly after delivery are cut away from paternal care.

The cruel procedure occurs because there is no money left in the pot once construction is completed for the establishment of a paternal authority. Instead, the management and maintenance of the building are shunted off to a municipal or state bureaucracy that is overworked, underfunded and too often politically appointed.

There never has been or will be a building designed and built without flaws that become apparent only after the structure is completed and used.

There are very legitimate justifications for changes after completion, such as the need for more convenient access to a stage, the redirection of ventilation outlets to make working areas usable, and the installation of stair railings to meet city building codes. Then, there are unreasonable alterations that emanate from the occupants who like to play architect and view a blank unused wall as a space for a door leading more directly to a corridor or lavatory.

Architects aren't guiltless, for whenever a designer ignores the necessity to provide adequate seating or trash receptacles, he extends an open invitation to every amateur decorator to improvise. As a former builder of store buildings, I observed similar situations, only it was buyers and merchants who were attempting to usurp architectural authority.

...lly, I solved the problem by declaring that our building might be motherless but not fatherless and that I, as the designated father, would accept all change suggestions and after a six-month interval would submit them to the architect for his response.

If he agreed, he was asked to submit his solution to the problem; if he didn't, the matter would revert back to my office, where it would be discussed in detail and a solution reached. In all cases, though, the architect would be given the courtesy to defend his original design—which is basic good manners and good design policy. At any rate, it cuts down on hasty improvisations.

This is a worldwide problem as far as public buildings are concerned. Just recently, I learned that the Fragrant Hills Hotel outside of Peking had fallen into complete disrepair through maintenance negligence. The Chinese officials have invited the original design team of architect I. M. Pei, textile designer Jack Lenor Larsen and decorator Dale Keller to return to Peking and strip the building to its basic structure before rehabilitating it. An adequate repair budget administered by a sympathetic building mother would have made the expensive restoration unnecessary.

I have sympathy with the government building supervisors who may be excellent custodians of maintenance funds. At times, they have been known to make one engineer responsible for the safety of elevator operations in six different buildings in various parts of town. When an elevator gets stuck with twelve passengers, it may take thirty minutes to two hours before the engineer is able to get to the site.

That is when a building yearns for a mother or father.
December 3, 1996

We Need Lessons in Humility

In a shop in Japan a few decades ago, I became aware of a brash, young American who was loud, boisterous and excessively demanding of the store's staff. He spoke in a strident voice and interrupted other customers who were conversing with the sales staff.

He even snatched objects out of the hands of those making purchases, saying "I want that!" The shop owner stood paralyzed, refusing to interfere with this obnoxious individual. It was obvious that the young man had been a large buyer, which, of course, was not an adequate excuse for his bad behavior.

As an American traveling abroad, I felt embarrassed that a fellow countryman was behaving so badly; the other Americans who were in the shop at the time cringed at this demonstration of boorishness. We all felt that this was a living demonstration of a book that had been published the year previously, *The Ugly American*. Months later, I learned that his father had gone to Japan to take his son home, where he was placed under mental supervision.

This unhappy incident reminded me of a tale involving another young American. The story to which I refer is about a college junior, traveling in Italy, who tried to absorb as much history and local atmosphere as quickly as possible. He breezed through Bologna in two hours. He blitzed Florence in a record-breaking day and a half; Parma and Sicily took two hours each. Venice slowed him down, for gondolas are not very speedy. He knocked off Rome in a day; Naples was so crowded that he was reduced to a crawl, but by fast driving in Sicily, he circled the island in two days.

een told of an important monastery in a small village of Sorrento, described by a friend as the most beautiful in Italy. It was a hard day's drive, but an hour after dusk he reached its gates. There were no lights, no sign of habitation.

He beat heavily on the stout wooden doors. There was no response. He rang the bell, and eventually he heard a voice inquiring in Italian, "Who's there?"

"A traveler," he replied. "I want to see the abbot."

"But he has retired."

"Wake him up, it's very important. I don't have much time."

Finally, the abbot appeared and inquired the reason for this urgent, nocturnal visit. The collegian, in a rush, said, "I've heard that this is a famous monastery. What are you famous for? Every monastic order has its specialty, I know, but I have no idea what is your specialty, and I'm in a great hurry to see your place and get on with my trip."

"My son," the abbot said, "it's too late to see our monastery, for the brothers are all asleep. Return tomorrow, and we will be happy to show you our simple abode."

"No, I'll be far gone by then," was the reply.

The abbot looked up at him sympathetically, and said, "Unlike the Benedictines, we're not known for our liqueurs. Unlike the Franciscans, we are not known for our charities. Unlike the Jesuits, we are not famous for our educators. But, my young American friend, we are known for something I fear you will never understand. We are known for our humility."

November 19, 1991

❧

Feelings of Superiority Are Laughable

What do you feel superior about? Deep in their hearts, all people believe that something they have, do or think is right, and they view with contempt those who haven't, don't, or disagree. Did you ever stop to think they feel the same way about you?

There's an awful lot of wasted contempt going on. Picture, for example, the exchange of glances between two drivers at a stoplight. One is at the wheel of an old but serviceable station wagon, and the other drives a brand-new supercharged Firesnorter, complete with extra chrome, airspoiler, multiple carburetors and a paint job that features gleaming teeth in Day-Glo colors.

The car enthusiast feels contempt for the suburbanite, thinking the poor slob probably doesn't even turn that pile of junk more than once a year. The suburbanite, meanwhile, is pitying the car enthusiast, not only for his misplaced value system, but for his deplorable taste.

Intellectuals are just as bad. Suppose an English professor writes a best-selling but trashy novel. While he's cashing his royalty checks and negotiating movie rights, he feels vastly superior to his academic colleagues who are still struggling to get their critiques of *Wuthering Heights* published in some obscure, scholarly journal. They, on the other hand, are staggering around puffed with pride that they haven't sold out their literary standards for anything so fleeting as fame and fortune.

Then there's the homeowner with his perfectly manicured lawn who feels contemptuous toward the man next door who has a crabgrass-infested yard, who in turn feels superior in the knowledge that his five miles a day jogging keeps him fit while the lawn-tender neighbor gets flabby.

Nowhere does a sense of superiority demonstrate itself more blatantly than when wine aficionados gather at a tasting event. One taster scoffs at the opinion of another about the bouquet and in turn is censored by another participant for his comments about the tannic acid content. Some of the remarks are valid; more often, they are attempts at creating an impression of superior knowledge.

If we'd stop to realize that the other fellow not only doesn't want to be in our shoes, but actually pities us for wearing them, we could all have a good laugh over the ultimate futility of intolerance in any form.

August 22, 1989

えへ

Standardization Limits Our Choices

For some years, observers of our society have been concerned with the growing standardization of products. It is becoming evident in a wide variety of industries.

Although the Industrial Revolution started in England with the invention of the steam engine more than 200 years ago, its effects on the production and distribution systems of industrialized nations still are becoming more and more obvious. In order to maximize products, factories are under pressure to standardize the design of products, whether they be automobiles or houses, women's dresses or personal computers.

Highly competitive marketers like Marks and Spencer in England limit the number of styles of garments and accessories they carry. That reduction of styles enables them to buy in greater depth in the colors and sizes they choose to stock. Their experience proves to them that restricted styles result in higher profits. (Shoppers in this country find greater assortments of products than in similar stores in Western Europe. Critics of our production methods point out that our vast variety is achieved only by a wasteful system, leading to higher prices or decreased profits.)

In the '80s, automakers produced dozens of models. But when the Japanese introduced a new type of intensive competition, American car manufacturers were forced to study every possible product economy they could achieve. That resulted in a standardization of models. And that in turn led to higher profits but less variety in the look of automobiles.

194

In a recent book review, columnist Rick Koster commented on the standardization that already is visible in book publishing: "It appears now that the marketing trend of the big publishing houses is to pump big bucks into one or two superstar authors, hype them unmercifully in the fashion of John Grisham, Stephen King and Michael Crichton, and, thereby, guarantee astronomical sales from the start. The other side of that strategy is that publishers will less often search out and nurture new talent."

That same concern was expressed in a recent *Wall Street Journal* piece by G. Bruce Knight, who wrote, "The superstores (like Borders, and Barnes and Noble) are largely responsible for the book industry's current plight. While the amount of retail space is growing at an unprecedented pace, sales haven't begun to pick up. In fact, sales of adult hardcover books, which have grown modestly in recent years, fell 4.4 percent last year. More still, while superstores order thousands of books, they devote most of their marketing muscle and prime shelf space to a relatively small number of potential best sellers."

Thus, we are witnessing a reduction in the variety of products from dresses to books, automobiles to ideas. We can't legislate against a trend, but we, as individuals, can encourage pluralism, a philosophy that espouses many ideas rather than just a few. More can be better.

June 17, 1997

ꝫ

Lying Just Gets You into More Trouble

"No, Joey, never lie. Lying just gets you into more trouble. Your dad would have told you the same thing if he were living, but since he isn't, I am telling you for him.

"Joey, I remember how, when you were 6 years old, you asked your dad, 'Is there really a Santa Claus?' and he told you, 'Yes, son, there is a spirit we call Santa Claus who comes once a year to reward boys and girls all over the world.' He wasn't telling you a lie; he was relating a myth of love and affection, of appreciation and warmth, that is such an important part of human society.

"I know you see many grown-ups who make statements that you know aren't true, and you may have seen them destroyed by their lies. It may not pay to tell the truth, but I know it doesn't pay to lie—even though you hear lies all around you, being told by the famous and the not so famous.

"Why do men and women lie? Because they think they can free themselves from embarrassing or illegal circumstances. They rarely succeed in the long run, because the truth usually will come out by accident or by intensive public exposure. When that occurs, liars have to defend not only their latest lie but the original subject they were trying to conceal, making it even worse than it would have been if they had just 'come clean' in the first place.

"Joey, when you read the newspapers, you are apt to find stories about important figures in all sorts of occupations, from politics and business to education and entertainment, who make some moral or legal mistake that they try to evade by telling a lie.

"Of course, there are a few lies that might be argued as justifiable, such as when an aged member of the family isn't told the whole truth about the fatal illness of a loved one.

"At present the American public has focused its attention on the allegations of President Clinton's extramarital activities and seems to have placed the importance of veracity behind the nation's prosperity. It appears that prosperity is outweighing the moral value of truthfulness. I am glad that you have noticed this and that you have brought it into focus.

"The discussion may help you through this critical moment in history. Remember Homer's account in the *Odyssey* of Achilles, the great Greek hero, who had one spot in his heel that was vulnerable to the arrow of his enemy or to his own carelessness.

"Joey, I hope this helps you through the period when you may see heroes fall. Remember that even heroes of today have a little spot in their heels that can be hit by a well-aimed arrow, as in the lore of ancient Greece."

February 17, 1998

ટે

Sometimes it Takes Laws to Enforce Ethics

"Ethics" is a word signifying how people and society respond to questions of right and wrong regarding moral values and political choices. It is one of the most useful indicators of how we, as individuals, are leading our daily lives and how we, as a nation, are drifting.

Ethics shouldn't be a racially dividing issue at this point in civilized man's history. It isn't a matter of black and white and brown and yellow, since we all benefit from good ethics and are damaged by bad ethical decisions.

The important state measures and municipal ordinances on ethical subjects were originally met with scorn and ridicule by some. The opponents of reforms, who had vigorously enriched their own pocketbooks, resisted the legislation that would protect the average citizen's interests.

Congress, in its unfathomable reasoning, does what many municipal governments do by permitting legislators to extend special privileges to a chosen few. Such unethical conduct is, of course, directly opposite to the public weal.

If such procedures were conducted in the daylight of public openness, it would be one thing. But when they are introduced without adequate public hearing, voters shake their heads and remember the old bit of wisdom, "You can't beat City Hall."

Recently, Dallas City Council member Laura Miller proposed changes that would place limits on former city officials' ability to accept jobs with companies that do business with the city. Both she and council member Donna Blumer questioned the appropriateness of former City Manager John Ware's going to work with Tom Hicks so soon after the two men negotiated the sports arena deal.

Last month, the mayor and other council members decided to delay a review of the ethics standards for the city. Ms. Miller, while supporting the delay, publicly advocates a vote on the ethics issue, not just the informal discussion. Conditions are such that pressure from constituents on their representatives to talk about ethics may be the only way of influencing them to take the high road.

None of this is new. Ethics has been talked about by every society from biblical days to the current times. We used to have the habit of overcoming inertia by excusing it as something that would have to wait until the next millennium. Now, that event is just around the corner.

Ethical conduct still remains the single most important element to bond humans, teams, business leadership and political forces. It hasn't been easy for the past 2,000 years. But from all indications, it faces an enlightened road ahead.

September 8, 1998

ॐ

Clinton Forces Us to Stand on Principles

"Dear Stanley:

"I am outraged when I read of the White House shenanigans, clever defense strategies and political hopscotching. I am confused and disturbed. Maybe you could put this into a historical context."

That opening paragraph, from a letter from a 28-year-old grandson, is a typical query being asked not only by young people, but by Americans of all ages. I hope this reply will provide some peace of mind for him and the millions like him.

Superficially, it looks as if there are three possible solutions—impeachment, censure or approbation. Americans have indicated through national polls that they want the president to finish out his term. Although that is a questionable decision, lawmakers will be loath to force him out of office.

Over the years, the presidency has been in the hands of a variety of human beings—from scoundrels to seers. So strong is our Constitution that the nation has remained intact despite the quality of the individual occupying the White House.

As the oldest practicing democracy in the world, we have been able to overcome the weaknesses of some of our leaders whom the electorate mistakenly voted into office. In my judgment, our democracy becomes strengthened by our ability to treat all citizens on an equal basis; in doing so, we have balanced the scales of justice.

However, this is the first time we have had a penitent sinner in the presidency—a man who has admitted his sins publicly and has made belated apologies to all of those affected by his sinning. It seems to many that the president, after a reluctance to admit his sins, is becoming guilty of plain, ordinary "chutzpah" or arrogance. He is seeking forgiveness as he asks for the opportunity to finish the job he has ignored in past months.

No chief executive officer of an educational institution or a company could expect to receive a pat on the back for ending up in the scandal sheets. We can forgive the president for his missteps, but we shouldn't reward him for having become a sinner, however repentant he may be. He has humiliated us before our friends in the major governments of the world, as well as before all the citizens, young and old, of our country. His misdeeds are commonly discussed by schoolchildren.

When he ran for office in 1992, he was in the midst of a sex scandal that the voters chose to sweep under the rug, so taken were they with the youthful vigor he presented. Well, the voters made a mistake, myself included. They have found out that his kind of leadership has produced some good results that have been overwhelmed by his personal deficiencies.

The time has come for Americans to stand up for the principles they teach their children—honesty, truthfulness and dependability.

The kids who have gotten into this story in a big way are completely confused. Each of us should be prepared to answer our children's questions, such as: "Should we do what you tell us to do—or what the president has done?"
September 22, 1998

EATHER

Weather Lore Isn't All Wet

If fat squirrels, red skies and mackerel clouds sound like a bad dream, then you obviously need to brush up on your down-home weather lore.

Low-flying bats, rainbows in the west, aching teeth, mackerel skies, fat squirrels, sun dogs, red skies at night, and croaking frogs all have something in common. They are staples of weather lore. Some of it is as old as the Bible, but it is also as modern as today's amateur meteorologists.

With today's modern, computerized weather equipment, we may likely scoff at ancient weather sayings. Our skyscraper offices and temperature-controlled houses keep us nicely insulated, but the early farmers and ancient mariners who depended on them for their safety and livelihoods may have the last laugh yet, because a lot of these cornball forecasts are actually based on scientific facts.

For example, a ring around the moon does mean that rain will come, usually within twenty-four hours. A line around a car wash often produces the same result. On a spring or fall evening, vapor rising from a river means that frost is coming. This does not apply, however, to mist rising from heated swimming pools. A morning rainbow in the west has nothing scientific to do with midgets or witches, but it does mean that rain is coming soon.

You can count on a January thaw—especially if an ice storm snaps the power lines to your deep freezer. And, last, frogs do croak more just before rain, but I can tell you from personal experience that crickets chirp more after they're inside the house!

Our nightly exposure to the professional weather forecasts on TV is having the effect of dulling our observation of nature's signals.

We prefer to watch the weather recap being explained with apparent authority by a commentator who appears to be an expert. Since no credentials are offered prior to the forecasts, I believe it's wise to be a bit skeptical until the announcer proves to be right at least three out of four broadcasts.

Weather lore is more than a lot of hot air, even if most of the predictions are accurate only to within twenty-four hours. But so what? Accurate predictions are often beyond the scope of professional meteorologists, too.

The public's obsession with weather reports has always puzzled me. Aside from knowing whether rain or snow is predicted, I find very little actual value that the information provides.

August 7, 1990

ORK

When Work Becomes Our Leisure

I once asked a contented farmer how it was that he enjoyed his work so much. "It's not work," he said, "unless you'd rather be doing something else at the time." The way we use our leisure time reminds me of his wise words.

Social critics are noticing lately that although we have shorter work hours and more labor-saving devices than ever, we always feel pressured for time. One reason is the way we use our leisure time, and I do mean *use*. We're involved in all sorts of time- and energy-consuming projects, from exercise classes to making our own macaroni.

The experts say it comes from increased leisure, pointing to the rise of the do-it-yourself fad in the postwar decade. Knee-deep in brick work from the new barbecue in the back yard, or sawdust from the new bookshelves in the den, white-collar men begin doing for pleasure what they are designed to do for pay.

Now, as women have entered the work force in the same capacities, we are seeing a similar phenomenon. There is a renewed interest in the things our mothers and grandmothers felt well out of—bread making, pickling, preserving and gourmet cooking from scratch. These things were work to our forebears, but we're simply doing them for play.

I don't think the trend is explained by a simple need to fill empty hours. A full day at the office and the commute home don't leave many. I think my farmer friend's attitude has more to do with it. When we had to do such projects, they were work, but now as more of us work with our heads, there's nothing we'd rather be doing than laboring with our hands.

The basic truth is that the demands on our time have vastly increased in the past fifty years. We are offered a wide variety of entertainment opportunities that weren't as prevalent several generations ago, such as lecture and concert courses, television, community meetings, volunteer services.

With all of the scientific achievements of this century that have increased the demands on our time, no brilliant inventor has found the way of increasing the length of the day, which still remains at twenty-four hours, nor any successful plan to reduce substantially the number required for sleep.

We may be driving ourselves to distraction to find enough hours in the day to fit in physical activity, but we're gaining in the long run to rediscover our need to satisfy our old-fashioned notion of an honest day's work.

December 27, 1988

A Basic Writing Lesson

As a result of my having written a few books which have been published, prospective authors frequently ask me for writing tips. I'm happy to oblige, because there are only a few basics, quickly told.

First, brush up on your grammar and spelling. Maybe you were the editor of your school paper and made all A's in English 101. You will still benefit from a no-nonsense little grammar book that is fun to read and the best in its field. It is *The Elements of Style* by William Strunk, Jr., and E. B. White.

Next, study the masters of prose. Because language is a living process, the novels of a modern master such as Saul Bellow bear little surface resemblance to the novels of Henry Fielding, but a deeper glance will reveal that both are craftsmen of the sentence. I urge you to become the same. Any form of creative expression worthy of survival is constantly changing, and writing is no exception.

The innovator needs a foundation in his craft before he begins to experiment. Pablo Picasso knew how to paint a face that looked like a face before he began to switch around noses and eyes. Learn to appreciate style in others before you insist on one of your own. Two writers, among many others, are outstanding in the manner in which they handle the English language. One is the American author John Hersey, who is a master of simplicity and clarity. The other is John le Carré, the pre-eminent British writer of espionage novels, whose best sellers have a style as rich and nourishing as a piece of fruitcake that has been soaked in port wine.

A good way to become aware of style is to read, one after another, several works by the same author. By the third or fourth book, you'll be noticing automatically the tricks of his trade. Notice why you can tolerate large doses of one author and why another quickly cloys or irritates.

Finally, discipline yourself to a regular writing schedule. I learned this lesson from my novelist friend, the late Irwin Shaw. Irwin was somewhat of a night owl and was noted for his late nocturnal habits. I asked him how he could stay up all night carousing and still be able to write the following day. His reply was, "No matter what time I get to bed or how much wine I've drunk, I'm always at my typewriter the next morning at 7 a.m. I write till noon, and what I do with the rest of the day is my own business."

He went on to say, "If you are going to write, you have to set a definite writing schedule—whether it be morning, afternoon, or night—and religiously stick to it. If you don't, you'll never produce anything." This was the best advice I ever received.

A final tip for would-be writers is to develop a tolerance for bad coffee. If your book is sold, you'll have to go on the early-morning talk-show circuit, and I can testify that television stations serve the worst coffee in the world.

February 19, 1991

∂❧

Every Writer Wins Some, Loses Some

Invariably at cocktail or dinner parties, I get collared by a fellow guest who confides that he always reads my columns in *The Dallas Morning News* and, although he enjoys them, he doesn't always agree with me.

My reply is that I'm glad he likes them, but I would be very unhappy if he or other readers agree with all my viewpoints. I go on to explain that if my columns were universally liked, I'd be writing a lot of piffle.

Agreement with a column is easy; disagreement requires an intellectual effort to buttress the reasons for dissent. If my columns activate readers to read critically, I have accomplished my objective. I don't seek agreement when I write, for my objective is to inform, clarify, expose fresh ideas and stimulate.

Other questions I am asked are: "How do you pick your topics? How long does it take to write a column? Who are your readers?"

To answer them, I have to go back to the genesis of my writing activities. After the publication of my books, *Minding the Store* and *Quest for the Best*, I was invited to be a commentator on a daily program for a local radio station. My broadcast was limited to 120 seconds, during which I had to make an opening statement that was provocative enough to catch the attention of the listeners, then a core topic that was interesting enough to hold them, and a brief finale to wrap it up.

The assignment forced me to write economically, for 120 seconds go by very quickly and the writer must be able to express himself clearly with minimum words. This experience has been most useful in writing a compact column that doesn't require too much of the reader's time, but leaves something to be remembered. A newspaper is filled with competitive attractions—other columns, breaking news stories, comics and horoscopes—and I think the compactness of my column is one of the reasons it has caught on.

Subjects come from reading newspapers and magazines, they are suggested by friends, and some of them are inspired by conversations with people who drop an idea that I think is column-worthy.

It takes me about forty-five minutes to write a piece, and then an hour or two to edit and polish it. An old advertising manager cautioned me, "Easy to write, hard to read; hard to write, easy to read." That's been a useful adage to remember.

My readers come from every walk of life, from garage parkers to lawyers, businessmen to restaurant waiters. Frequently, I am stopped in the street by strangers who simply say, "I liked your column yesterday," or, "You sure lost me on that one."

In my eleventh year as a columnist, I still enjoy the opportunity that writing gives me to express my opinions. Most of all, I appreciate my readers, whoever and wherever they are, for the acceptance and support.

July 27, 1995

కు

Writing Easier Than Selling

Writing a book is relatively easy; selling it is the more arduous task. I made that discovery when my first book, *Minding the Store*, came out in 1974. I am finding that nothing has changed now that a new edition of the book has been issued as a feature of Neiman Marcus' 90th birthday celebration.

I shouldn't have been surprised, for very little in a store sells without proper presentation, an aura of excitement and adequate publicity. In the case of books, it is necessary to differentiate a single title from the 12,000 others that are published and distributed every six months.

So to sell my book, I have to go on the road, appear on TV programs and repeat my family history to inquiring reporters who need a tale of sorts on which to hang their story. That can become pretty dull, but that is part of the drill required to make your book sell in the cruel world of literature.

There is one part of a book tour that I do enjoy. It is the autographing session in which the author is lucky if he meets a continuous stream of customers. Don't knock it; that is the sizzle on the steak platter. A long line of people waiting for a signed book stimulates others to get in line, too, and buy a book.

One of the more interesting aspects of the autographing session is that the author has no idea of how many different ways there are to spell some customers' names—like Ruth Ann, which can vary from Reuth Ann to Ruttie Anne to Ruth Enn. That holds true for scores of names. An autographer learns quickly that it is unwise to "wing it" by guessing the spelling, so he asks the customer to write the proper spelling on a piece of paper. That can save many books from being mutilated.

A writer encounters all sorts of zany requests, such as "To Ruttie Anne—I love you." That, you explain, is something the donor can say but not the author, unless he happens to know the recipient. Even then, it is dangerous because the husband may take exception to such a declaration.

Then there is the buyer who has written an inscription that runs several hundred words. Invariably, such a buyer appears just as you are trying to finish the session so that you can make the plane to your next destination.

The most unusual demand I have encountered took place in Houston when a customer, who was introduced to me as having just purchased a stunning Galanos dress, asked that I inscribe her book to her husband, "Hank, I just found the evening dress of my dreams. The emeralds are on the first floor. Love Suzi."

I got the message. I hope Hank did, too.

October 7, 1997

ESTERDAY

Our Ancestors Weren't Dumb

For some reason we persist in the belief that mankind is getting smarter, more humane and more technologically expert. I hope this is so, but the jury is still out while new evidence to the contrary accumulates.

We shudder at the historical accounts of the excesses of Attila the Hun, and conveniently forget that we are the generation of Adolf Hitler, Hiroshima and Saddam Hussein. We decry the scorched-earth practices of dictators, yet we practice carpet bombing in sorties against our enemies. We exult in our triumph over tuberculosis and smallpox while ignoring the epidemic of cancer in our midst, brought on in part by self-administered and commercially produced poisons. We laugh at our ancestors' worship of sun and thunder while we are helplessly immobilized by winter storms and summer floods.

This intellectual chauvinism is so powerful that it's kept us from figuring out how the Egyptians built the pyramids, even though the evidence has been right under our noses for years. Our refusal to give these ancient technicians credit for their engineering expertise made us ready, at one time, to believe that spacemen, or divine intervention, hoisted the tons of stones to the top of those beautifully designed tombs.

An article in *Discovery* magazine disclosed that an engineer named John Bush took a fresh look at some wooden rockers found in Egypt by archaeologists and made some startling experiments to buttress his thesis. Flat on top and semicircular on bottom, four of these rockers could be attached to a block of stone to form a wheel-shaped cylinder, Mr. Bush reasoned. To prove his point, he did just that with replicas he made. He attached them to a 4,500-pound concrete block. Then, with the aid of a rope and seven other men, he hoisted the block up a 25-foot incline in less than two minutes.

The importance of this experiment is that it highlights our tendency to underestimate the brainpower of early man.

We in the 20th century have been inclined to give too little credit to the intellectual capability of our forebears, who, with primitive instruments and vast resources of manpower, succeeded in achieving some remarkable accomplishments.

One of the primary causes for our underestimation of early man may be attributed to the difference we have placed on the valuation of time. We are educated to regard the number of hours spent in any endeavor as vital as a cost factor, simply because we have so many alternative uses for time. For a people not in a hurry to go anywhere, time had little worth comparable to today's valuation. A huge architectural project or a transmigration across continents carried no promised delivery date.

The important criteria was the value of the project to the society that was willing to dedicate the time necessary for achievement of its goal.

Scientists tell us that our brains are no different from those of the original Homo sapiens. Frankly, I'm flattered to think that I have the same mental equipment as Homer, Hammurabi and the unknown genius who domesticated fire.

May 14, 1991

Zoos Finally Give Animals a Break

Heraclitus, the 5th-century B.C. Greek philosopher, declared that the only certainty in life was flux. Humans accepted this dictum but have fought change, nonetheless.

In this century we have witnessed more flux, or change, than any other like period of time has produced, and we're having difficulty keeping up with continuing changes in all phases of life—in education, finance, medicine, you name it.

An abbreviation, zoo, from zoological society, used to refer to parks divided into pens where strange and wondrous creatures from around the world were housed in captivity for the education of young humans. There, many of the animals, while being observed and surreptitiously fed, were deprived of their previous freedom to roam and frolic as they had in their native habitats.

In the mid-20th century, zookeepers began to rethink their solutions and came up with ideas of how to re-establish environments more comparable with nature. A very good demonstration of this concept is the four-acre African savanna that has been constructed in Toledo, Ohio, which contains the world's only underwater viewing area for hippopotami.

The Hippoquarium is a 360,000-gallon pool that permits the zoo's two Nile hippos to swim right up to the visitors on the other side of the glass and stare them in the eye, or meet them nose to nose. The savanna also allows various African animals—such as elephants, rhinos and meerkats—to roam in naturalistic areas that resemble their grassland habitat.

Dallas now boasts the Wilds of Africa, a 25-acre addition to the Dallas Zoo featuring six major African habitats. Instead of trudging on trails, visitors can observe from the vantage point of a monorail ninety species of birds, mammals and reptiles in surroundings that imitate their natural surroundings. A nature trail is also available at the conclusion of the monorail ride.

To top it all, there's the Jake L. Hamon Gorilla Conservation Research Center, a two-acre preserve for the zoo's lowland gorillas. Long-range plans call for the enlargement of the Wilds of Africa to 55 acres, more than doubling the size of the present zoo.

The changes that have come about in zoos, thanks to private philanthropy and public funding, give both the public and the animals a break. Both will look at each other differently.

May 1, 1990

Epilogue

It's Been a Good 15 ½ Years of Columns

Fifteen-and-half years ago, *The Dallas Morning News* invited me to write a regularly scheduled column for its op-ed page. I replied by saying, "I can handle a once-a-week piece and would enjoy the assignment." I also stipulated that I would write about any subject I deemed appropriate from politics and sports to literature and etymology. The editors graciously agreed.

So, during those 15 1/2 years that I have been writing for the Viewpoints page, I have ventured to criticize customer service, Southern Methodist University's patronage of athletes for its various sports teams, and the foibles and duplicity of the president of the United States. Reports on new eating places were popular, as were the columns on the continuing importance of good manners in expressing appreciation for gifts or courtesies.

As I look back, I think that I was, and still am, obsessed with the forces of change that are challenging our society as never before. More and more, I am convinced that change is one of the natural characteristics of an organized society and that it needs to be received with open minds and understanding. This atmosphere of change isn't temporary; it will be a part of our lives forevermore, just as the seasons force nature to change the color of leaves.

For better or worse, the computer is with us, and it, too, will change as creative minds mold it into a tool that can be of greater service and utility. Those who carry over 19th-century preferences can moan and groan, but hand wringing won't impede the marketing and use of new tools that provide more information and better comprehension of the world in which we live.

My motivation in accepting this role as a columnist was to help people deal with change and to take note of the variety of interesting things in life that so often get lost because of the competition for our time. It is pleasing to me that so many people who have read my column have taken the time to express their feelings to me by word of mouth and written notes.

The best compliment I ever received came from a stranger who recently stopped me in a restaurant and asked, "Are you Stanley Marcus?" I replied, "To my best knowledge, I am." "Well, I have been reading you for the past 15 years, and I rarely agree with you. But don't stop, keep it up because you gradually are breaking down the rigidity of my thinking."

If I have succeeded in that accomplishment, I can retire from the job of a weekly columnist to that of an occasional contributor to this page.

November 2, 1999

Index

Volume I
The Viewpoints of Stanley Marcus: A Ten-year Perspective

manners
in gift giving, 103–4, 117–18
lack of, in business education, 57–58
scarcity of, 87–88
teaching, 33–34, 41–42
maps, 213–14
Marcus, Herbert, 221–22
marketing
changes in department
stores, 211–12
emotional appeals in, 111–12
of Native American
blackware, 185–86
promoting customer service,
245–46
during recessions, 209–10
terminology of, 131–32
Marriage of Heaven and Hell
(Blake), 116
marriages
advice regarding, 232
arranged, 35–36
effect of relocation on, 233–
34
second, 117–18
Martin, Judith, 33
Marxhausen, Reinhold, 98
mass production, 63, 141–43
McDermott, Eugene, 221
McGraw, Bill, 4
media
coverage of educational
crisis, 123–24
depiction of business
leaders, 53–54
fashion press, 16–17
inconsistency in coverage,
44
promotion of "newspeak,"
22

use of stereotypes in, 14–15
Medina, Edith, 223
mediocrity, 156–57
memory retention, 97–98
Mencken, H. L., 95–96
Menuhin, Diana, 25
merchandising
changes in department
stores, 211–12
gardening analogy, 146–47
inventory control, 39–40
luxury goods, 141–43
Native American blackware,
185–86
seasonal clearances, 197–98
mergers, effect on communities, 139–40
merit pay, 123–24
Merrymount Press, 111
Michelangelo, 30
A Midsummer Night's Dream
(Shakespeare), 177
military spending, 39–40
miniature books, 166–67
Miss Manners (Judith Martin),
33
Moore, Henry, 29
moralism, 243–44
mourning, 179–80
myths in retailing, 211–12

N

National Collegiate Athletic
Association (NCAA)
court rulings regarding, 8
recruiting rules of, 44
National Commission on
Excellence, 123–24
National Recovery Administra-
tion, 176

public ownership of businesses, 63, 82
public service, 65–66, 67–68
publicity, Santa Fe Indian Market, 185–86
publishing, 166–67, 213
Pucci, Marchese de, 201

𝒬

quality
    appraising, 69–70, 187–88, 193–94
    in customer service, 111–12
    decline in, 63, 141–43
    quality control in building industry, 247–49
    value of, 205
Quest for the Best (Marcus), 81, 238

ℛ

racism, 101–2
reading, 193–94
reading glasses, 129–30
Reagan, Ronald
    attitude toward the homeless, 174
    deregulation, 136
    JAL crash, 50
    passing of blame, 23
    tax increases, 21
recessions
    arts funding during, 252–53
    consumer habits during, 254–55
    marketing during, 209–10
    self discipline during, 203–4
red tape in health care, 227–28
redbud trees, 62
regulations, 135–36

religious institutions, author criticized by, 7
relocation, 233–34
responsibility, presidential, 23–24
restaurant business, quality issues in, 65–66
retailing
    attention to details, 225–26
    author's introduction to, 156–57
    myths in, 211–12
    retailers' role in defining taste, 260–61
    role in defining tastes, 260–61
    supply in retail environment, 40
returns, customer service regarding, 241–42
Ringling Brothers and Barnum and Bailey Circus, 200
risk, changing attitudes toward, 115–16
Rolls-Royce, 165
Rooney, Andy, 132
Roosevelt, Franklin D., 166, 175–76, 216
Ross, Steve, 221
routine's effect on creative process, 92
rules, 135–36
rural living, 217–18
Ruskin, John, 188

𝒮

St. Lawrence River, 213
salesmanship
    contrasted with order filling, 137–38
    customer service and, 160–61

Index

Stanley Marcus from A to Z
Viewpoints Volume II

Dallas Museum of Art, 27, 135

Dallas Times Herald, 28

Dealey, George Bannerman, 125–126

The Decision Makers/The Power Structure of Dallas (Thometz), 57

Declaration of Independence, 64

democracy, Churchill quote on, 106

Dent, Alan, 128–129

designer clothing, 153

desks as indicator of personality, 61–62

diagnosis of illness, 66–67

Dibble's First Law of Sociology, 2

Dickens, Charles, 128

Dickinson, Emily, 128

Dickson, Paul, 1

The Dictionary of American Places, 184

dieting
    advice regarding, 31–32
    Dieter's Law, 2
    and fitness programs, 49–51
    Hayes Diet, 33
    kissing diet, 81–82
    low-fat cooking, 42–43
    variety of diets, 33–34

Diogenes's Second Dictum, 2

disabilities, 7–8

disagreements, settling, 59–60

discipline, 145–146

Discovery (magazine), 211

disease, advances in treating, 211–212

Disney, Walt, 185

Disney's Magic Kingdom, 185

divorce, 106

Don Quixote, 149

Dondero list, 28

Doran, Ed, 21

dreams, 35–36

dress
    casual Fridays, 39–40, 96–97
    designer clothing, 153
    fur coats, 162
    quality control in manufacturing, 155–156
    sizing, 49–50

The Dunciad, 128

E

e-mail, casual usage of language in, 96

Ecclesiastes
    predictions of, 131
    on silence, 103

economics, supply and demand, 23–24

Edinburgh Festival, 128

Edison, Thomas, 131

education
    legal battles over hair length, 12
    in retail business, 10
    value of, 5

efficiency, 45–47

elders, cultural references to, 136

electricity, predictions regarding, 131

The Elements of Style (Strunk and White), 205

Eliot, T. S., 128, 131

Emerson, Ralph Waldo, 129

Emerson's Law of Compensation, 55

Metro-Goldwyn-Mayer, 153–155
Metropolitan Museum, 27, 135
Mexican cuisine, 182
Michtom, Morris, 179–180
Middle Ages, music during, 108
Miller, Laura, 197–198
Minding the Store (Marcus),
207, 208
mink coats, 162
M&M/Mars, 42
models, changes in fashion, 50
money, shortcomings of
currency, 29–30
moon, 201
mortality, reminders of, 8
mother, author's, 9
motion picture business, 45–47
Mozart, 107
Mr. Smith Goes to Washington
(Capra), 115
municipal ordinances, 197
Muschamp, Herbert, 166
museums
critics of, 27
signs at, 135
music, 107–108

N

National Engineers Week, 76
NationsBank Plaza, 132
nature
flowers, 109–110
gardening, 55–56
predicting weather, 201–202
Nazi Party, predictions regarding, 131
neatness, 61–62
neighborhoods, zoning restrictions in, 111–112
Neiman Marcus Fortnight, 184

Nemmy, Enid, 104
New York Herald, 129
The New York Times
on accounting practices, 96–
97
architectural review, 166
book reviews, 17, 129
on marriage, 104
on motion picture industry,
45–47
on unrecognized talent, 171
on use of slang, 92
New York Times Book Review,
113
New Yorker magazine, 32
Newcastle, Simon, 130
News Chronicle, 129
Newsweek, 27
Nitot, 71
nonconformity, 113–114
North Dallas, 112
nouvelle cuisine, 42–44, 75

O

Oak Cliff, 125
obesity, 81–82. *See also* dieting
odds, 117–118
Odyssey, 196
The Official Rules (Dickson), 1
O'Keeffe, Georgia, 109
old age. *See* age
olive oil, 162–163
Olympics, 167–169
organization in Christmas
shopping, 164–165
Organization of Petroleum
Exporting Countries (OPEC),
132
Osborne, Burl, xi
overpricing, 175–176

𝒫

Padgett, Win, 89
painting, innovations in, 74–75
Parents Magazine, 53
Paris, France, 111, 167
Park Cities, 112
Peanuts, 141
Pei, I. M., 190
pencils, 118–119
The People's Almanac, 124
persecution, 27–28
perseverance, 172
personalities, evaluating, 118–119
philanthropy, 37, 213–214
phobias, 123–124
photography, 175
"physically challenged," use of term, 7–8
pianoforte, music for, 107–108
Picasso, Pablo, 205
planning for urban areas, 125–127
Plaza Hotel, 157
pluralism, 195
"A Pocketful of Turkish Proverbs" (pamphlet), 136
Pogo (cartoon), 91
politeness. *See* manners
political cartoons, 179
politics, ethics in, 197–198
Pollock, Jackson, 108
power structure in Dallas, 57–58
predictions
  from 1954, 131–132
  misguided, 128–129, 130–131
  regarding weather, 201–202
presidency, effect of scandals on, 198–200

press, influence on health issues, 50
pricing practices, 154–155, 175–176
Princeton Dental Resource Center, 41
Princeton University, 166–167
printing, 133–134
The Prisoner of Zenda (Hope), 184
private presses, 133–134
promotional events, 168
prophecy. *See* predictions
Proust, Marcel, 37–38
proverbs, 21–22, 136–137
psychoanalysis, 123
publicity for books, 208
publishing
  print size, 134–135
  private presses, 133–134
  Pushcart Press, 128
  standardization in, 195
punishment, 145–146
Pushcart Press, 128
pyramids, simulating building of, 211–212

𝒬

quality
  decline in, 156–158
  items exhibiting, 139–140
quality control programs, 155–156
Quest for the Best (Marcus), 3, 139, 173, 207

𝓡

radio
  author's commentary on, 207
  predictions regarding, 130